# GOD PROMISES YOU

## CHARLES SPURGEON

WHITAKER
HOUSE

Unless otherwise indicated, all Scripture quotations are taken from the King James Version (KJV) of the Bible.
Scripture quotations marked (RSV) are from the *Revised Standard Version Common Bible* © 1973, by the Division of Christian Education of the National Council of Churches of Christ in the USA. Used by permission.

Editor's note: This book has been edited for the modern reader. Words, expressions, and sentence structure have been updated for clarity and readability.

**GOD PROMISES YOU**

ISBN: 0-88368-685-6
Printed in the United States of America
© 1995 by Whitaker House

Whitaker House
30 Hunt Valley Circle
New Kensington, PA 15068
visit our web site at: www.whitakerhouse.com

Library of Congress Cataloging-in-Publication Data

Spurgeon, C. H. (Charles Haddon), 1834–1892.
  God promises you / By Charles Spurgeon.
      p. cm.
  ISBN 0-88368-685-6 (pbk.)
  1. Christian life—Baptist authors.  I. Title.
  BV4501.3 .S67 2001
  242—dc21

                                          2001003804

1 2 3 4 5 6 7 8 9 10 11 / 09 08 07 06 05 04 03 02

# CONTENTS

# CHAPTER ONE

# A SIEVE NEEDED

# ❧ 1 ❧
# A Sieve Needed

*For, lo, I will command, and I will sift the house of Israel among all nations, like as corn is sifted in a sieve, yet shall not the least grain fall upon the earth.*
—Amos 9:9

I t is very important to be able to distinguish between things that differ, for appearances are not to be relied upon. Things that seem to be alike may actually be the opposite of each other. A scorpion may be like an egg and a stone like a piece of bread, but they are far from being the same. Like may be very unlike. This is especially the case in spiritual things, and therefore it is to our advantage to be on our guard.

It would be very difficult to say how far a man may go in religion and yet die in his sins. He may very well look like an heir of heaven and yet be a child of wrath. Many unconverted men have a belief that is similar to faith, and yet it is not true faith. Certain people exhibit pious dispositions that have the warmth of spiritual love but are quite destitute of gracious life. Every grace can be counterfeited, even as jewels can be imitated. As paste gems are wonderfully like the real stones, so sham graces are marvelously like the work of the Spirit of God. In soul matters a man will need to have all his wits about him, or he will soon deceive his own heart. It is to be feared that many are already mistaken and will never discover their delusion until they lift up their eyes in the world of woe, where their disappointment will be terrible indeed.

The dead child of nature may be carefully washed by his mother, but this will not make him a living child of grace. The life of God within the soul creates an infinite difference between the man who has it and the man who does not. The point is to make sure that we have this life. Are you sure that you have it?

It will be an awful thing to cry, "Peace, peace," where there is no peace and to falsely prophesy smooth things for yourself. This may make your heart easy, but it could lull your conscience into a slumber. You might never wake out of the deep until a clap of the thunder of judgment startles you out of presumption into endless horror.

I desire to help you, my reader, in the business of self-examination. I actually want you to go further than examination. You need to realize that you can attain such an abundance of grace that your holy and happy state will become a witness to yourself.

# A Sieve Needed

The first part of this little book is meant to be a sieve to separate the chaff from the wheat. Use it upon yourself. It may be the best day's work you have ever done. He who looked into his accounts and found that his business was a losing one was saved from bankruptcy. This may happen also to you. Should you, however, discover that your heavenly trade is prospering, it will be a great comfort to you. No man can ever lose by honestly searching his own heart. Friend, try it at once.

# CHAPTER TWO

## THE TWO SEEDS

# ≈ 2 ≈
# THE TWO SEEDS

*It is written, that Abraham had two sons, the one by a bondmaid, the other by a freewoman. But he who was of the bondwoman was born after the flesh; but he of the freewoman was by promise.*
—Galatians 4:22–23

Abraham had two sons, Ishmael and Isaac, who were beyond all dispute veritable sons of Abraham. Yet one of them inherited the covenant blessing, and the other was simply a prosperous man of the world. See how similar these two were to each other. They were born in the same society, called the same great patriarch "father," and sojourned in the same encampment with him. Yet Ishmael was a stranger to the covenant, while Isaac was the heir of the promise. How little is there in blood and birth!

A more remarkable instance than this happened a little afterward. Esau and Jacob were both born to the same mother, at the same birth, yet it is written, *"Jacob have I loved, but Esau have I hated"* (Rom. 9:13). One became gracious, and the other profane. So closely may two come together, and yet so widely may they be separated. Truly, it is not only true that these two will be in one bed and that one will be taken and the other left, but they will come into the world at the same moment. Yet one of them will take up his inheritance with God, and the other will sell his birthright for a morsel of meat. We may be in the same church, baptized in the same water, seated at the same communion table, singing the same psalm, and offering the same prayer, and yet we may be of two races as opposed as the seed of the woman and the seed of the serpent.

Abraham's two sons were declared by Paul to be the types of two races of men who are much alike and yet widely different. They are unlike in their origin. They were both sons of Abraham, but Ishmael, the child of Hagar, was the offspring of Abraham upon ordinary conditions. He was born after the flesh. Isaac, the son of Sarah, was not born by the strength of nature. His father was more than a hundred years old, and his mother was long past childbearing age. He was given to his parents by the Lord, and was born according to the promise through faith. This is a grave distinction, and it marks off the true child of God from him who is only so by profession. The promise lies at the bottom of the distinction, and the power that goes to accomplish the promise creates and maintains the difference. Hence, the promise that is our inheritance is also our test and touchstone.

Let us use the test at once by seeing whether we have been formed by the power that fulfills the promise. Let me ask a few questions: How were you converted? Was it by yourself, by the persuasion of men, by carnal excitement, or was it by the operation of the Spirit of God? You profess to have been born again. Where did that new birth come from? Did it come from God in consequence of His eternal purpose and promise, or did it come out of yourself? Was it your old nature trying to do better, and working itself up to its best form? If so, you are Ishmael. Or was it that you, being spiritually dead and having no strength whatever to rise out of your lost estate, were visited by the Spirit of God? Did God put forth His divine energy and cause life from heaven to enter into you? Then you are Isaac. All will depend upon the commencement of your spiritual life and the source from which that life at first proceeded. If you began in the flesh, you have gone on in the flesh, and in the flesh you will die.

Have you never read, *"That which is born of the flesh is flesh"* (John 3:6)? Before long the flesh will perish, and from it you will reap corruption. Only *"that which is born of the Spirit is spirit"* (v. 6). The joy is that the spirit will live, and of it you will reap life everlasting. Whether you profess to be religious or not, I beseech you, ask yourself, Have I felt the power of the Spirit of God?

Is the life that is within you the result of the fermentation of your own natural desires? Or is it a new element, infused, imparted, implanted from above? Is your spiritual life a heavenly creation?

Have you been created anew in Christ Jesus? Have you been born again by divine power?

Ordinary religion is nature gilded over with a thin layer of what is thought to be grace. Sinners have polished themselves up and brushed off the worst of the rust and the filth, and they think their old nature is as good as new. This touching-up and repairing of the old man is all very well, but it falls short of what is needed. You may wash the face and hands of Ishmael as much as you please, but you cannot make him into Isaac. You may improve nature, and the more you do so, the better for certain temporary purposes, but you cannot raise it into grace. There is a distinction at the very fountainhead between the stream that rises in the bog of fallen humanity and the river that proceeds from the throne of God.

Do not forget that our Lord Himself said, *"Ye must be born again"* (John 3:7). If you have not been born again from above, all your churchgoing or your chapel-going stands for nothing. Your prayers and your tears, your Bible readings, and all that has come from only yourself, can lead only to yourself. Water will naturally rise as high as its source but no higher. That which begins with human nature will rise to human nature, but it cannot reach to the divine nature. Was your new birth natural or supernatural? Was it of the will of man or of God? Much will depend upon your answer to that question.

Between the child of God and the one who merely professes to be so, there is a distinction of the most serious sort as to origin. Isaac was born according to promise. Ishmael was not of promise but of the course of nature. Where nature's strength suffices there is no promise, but when human energy fails, the Word of the Lord comes in. God had said that Abraham would have a son with Sarah. Abraham believed it and rejoiced therein, and Isaac was born as the result of the divine promise, by the power of God. There could have been no Isaac if there had been no promise. There can be no true believer apart from the promise of grace and the grace of the promise.

Gentle reader, here let me inquire as to your salvation. Are you saved by what you have done? Is your religion the product of your own natural strength? Do you feel equal to all that salvation may require? Do you conclude yourself to be in a safe and happy condition because of your natural excellence and moral ability? Then you are after the manner of Ishmael, and to you the inheritance will not come. It is not an inheritance according to the flesh but according to promise.

On the other hand, you may say: My hope lies only in the promise of God. He has set forth that promise in the person of His Son, Jesus, to every sinner who believes in Him. I do believe in Him; therefore, I trust and believe that the Lord will fulfill His promise and bless me. I look for heavenly blessedness not as the result of my own efforts but as the gift of God's free favor. My hope is fixed alone upon the free and gratuitous love of God to guilty men. He has given His Son Jesus Christ to put away sin and to bring in everlasting righteousness for those who do not deserve it.

This thinking is another sort of language from that of the Ishmaelites who say, *"We have Abraham to our father"* (Matt. 3:9). You have now learned to speak as Isaac speaks. The difference may seem small to the careless, but it is great indeed. Hagar, the slave-mother, is a very different person from Sarah, the princess. To the one, there is no covenant promise; to the other, the blessing belongs forevermore. Salvation by works is one thing; salvation by grace is another. Salvation by human strength is far removed from salvation by divine power. Salvation by our own resolve is the opposite of salvation by the promise of God.

Put yourself under this inquiry and see to which family you belong. Are you of Ishmael or of Isaac?

If you find that you are like Isaac, born according to the promise, remember that your name is "Laughter," for that is the interpretation of the Hebrew name Isaac. Take care that you *"rejoice with joy unspeakable and full of glory"* (1 Pet. 1:8). Your new birth is a wonderful thing. If both Abraham and Sarah laughed at the thought of Isaac, you may certainly do so concerning yourself. There are times when, if I sit alone and think of the grace of God to me, the most undeserving of all His creatures, I am ready to laugh and cry at the same time. I become joyous that the Lord would have ever looked in love and favor upon me. And every child of God must have felt the working of that Isaac nature within his soul, filling his mouth with laughter, because the Lord has done great things for him.

Mark well the difference between the two seeds from their very beginning. Ishmael comes from man and by man. Isaac comes by God's promise. Ishmael is the child of Abraham's flesh. Isaac is Abraham's child, too. Then the power of God comes in, and from the weakness of his parents it is made clear that he is of the Lord—a gift according to promise. True faith is assuredly the act of the man who believes. True repentance is the act of the man who repents. Yet both faith and repentance may with unquestionable correctness be described as the work of God. Isaac is the son of Abraham and Sarah, and yet he is still more the gift of God. The Lord our God, who entreats us to believe, also enables us to believe. All that we do acceptably the Lord works in us. The very will to do it is of His working. No religion that is not essentially the outflow of the man's own heart is worth a farthing. Yet it must beyond question be the work of the Holy Spirit who dwells within him.

O friend, if what you have within you is natural, and only natural, it will not save you! The inward work must be supernatural. It must come from God or it will miss the covenant blessing. A gracious life will be your own even as Isaac was truly the child of Abraham. Most importantly this life will be from God, for *salvation is of the* LORD" (Jonah 2:9). We must be born from above. Concerning all our religious feelings and actions, we must be able to say, "Lord, You have formed all our works in us."

# CHAPTER THREE

# THE TWO LIVES

# ❦ 3 ❦
# THE TWO LIVES

*Neither, because they are the seed of Abraham, are they*
*all children: but, In Isaac shall thy seed be called.*
*That is, They which are the children of the flesh,*
*these are not the children of God: but the children*
*of the promise are counted for the seed. For this is*
*the word of promise, At this time will I come,*
*and Sarah shall have a son.*
—Romans 9:7–9

Ishmael and Isaac differed as to origin, and hence there was a difference in their nature that showed itself in their lives. It was chiefly seen in their relation to the promise.

According to the birth, so will be the life that comes of it. In the case of the man who is only what he made himself to be, there will be only what nature gives him. In the case of the man who is created anew by the Spirit of God, there will be signs following.

*Of him are ye in Christ Jesus, who of God is made*
*unto us wisdom, and righteousness, and sanctifica-*
*tion, and redemption:...as it is written, He that glo-*
*rieth, let him glory in the Lord.*    (1 Cor. 1:30–31)

There will be in the newborn man that which the
new life brings with it. In the natural man there will
be nothing of the kind.

Ishmael exhibited some of the natural charac-
teristics of Abraham joined with those of his slave-
mother. He was a princely man like his father, and
he inherited the patriarch's noble bearing. Isaac had
the faith of his father, and he was in the succession
as to holy inward spiritual life. As the heir of the
promise, Isaac remained with his father Abraham,
while Ishmael was forming camps of his own in
the wilderness. Isaac sought alliance with the olden
stock in Mesopotamia. Ishmael's mother took him
a wife out of Egypt, which was very natural since
she came from Egypt herself. Like will to like. Isaac
meditated in the field at eventide, for his conversation was with sacred things. Ishmael contended with
all comers, for he minded earthly things. Meditation
is not for the wild man whose hand is against every
man and every man's hand against him. Isaac sur-
rendered himself as a sacrifice to God. You see nothing of that kind in Ishmael. Self-sacrifice is not for
Ishmael. He is rather a killer and a slayer than a
lamb that presents itself to God.

So you will find that if you are religiously trained
and tutored and become "pious," as they call it, and
yet are not renewed in heart or visited by the Holy

Spirit, you will not live the secret life of the child of God. You may show many of the outward marks of a Christian. You may be able to sing and to pray and to quote Scripture and perhaps to tell some little bits of imaginary experience, but you must be born again to know in very deed and truth the fellowship of the saints. You must also be born again to know communion in secret with the living God and the yielding of yourself to Him as your reasonable service.

The child of the promise abides with God's people and counts it his privilege to be numbered with them. The child of the promise feels that he is in the best company when no man can see or be seen because it is then that the Great Invisible draws near to him and holds conversation with him. The child of the promise, and he alone, is able to go up to the top of Moriah, there to be bound upon the altar and to yield himself up to God. I mean by this last example that only he who is born of the Spirit will yield himself wholly to God and love the Lord better than life itself. Your nature and conduct will be according to your origin. Therefore, I pray that you may begin aright, so that as you profess to be a child of the kingdom, you may prove to be a true-born heir.

Ishmael, who was born after the flesh, the child of the bondwoman, must always bear the servile taint. The child of a slave is not freeborn. Ishmael is not and cannot be what Isaac is—the child of the free woman. Now remember, I do not say that Ishmael ever desired to be like Isaac. I do not say that he felt himself to be a loser by differing from Isaac; but, indeed, he was so.

The man who is laboring for self-salvation by his own doings, feelings, and self-denials may be proudly ignorant of his servile state. He may even boast that he was born free and was never in bondage to any. Yet he spends his whole life in servitude. He never knows what liberty means, what contentment means, what delight in God means. He wonders when men talk about "full assurance of faith." He judges that they must be presumptuous. He has scarcely time to breathe between the cracks of the whip. He has done so much, but he must do so much more. He has suffered so much, but he must suffer so much more. He has never come into the rest that is promised for the people of God. He is born of the bondwoman, and his spirit is ever in bondage.

On the other hand, he who is born of the free woman understands that salvation is of the grace of God from first to last. He also knows that where God has given His grace He does not take it back, *"for the gifts and calling of God are without repentance"* (Rom. 11:29). Such a man, accepting the finished work of Christ and knowing his acceptance in the Beloved, rests in the Lord and rejoices exceedingly. His life and his spirit are filled with joy and peace for he was born free, and he is free, yes, free indeed.

Do you understand the freedom of the child of God? Or are you still in servitude under the law, afraid of punishment, afraid of being sent away into the wilderness? If you are in this latter case, you have not received the promise, or you would know that such a thing could not be. To Isaac, the child of the promise, the heritage belongs, and he abides forever without fear of being cast out.

Those who are born as Ishmael was, according to the flesh, and whose religion is a matter of their own power and strength, mind earthly things, as Ishmael did. Only those who are born from above through the promise according to faith will, like Isaac, mind heavenly things. See how the naturally religious man minds earthly things. He is very regular at his place of worship, but while he is there he thinks of his business, his house, or his farm. Does he enjoy the worship of God? Not he! There is a sermon. Does he receive with meekness the engrafted Word that is able to save his soul? Not he! He criticizes it as if it were a political harangue.

This naturally religious man gives his money to the cause of God as others do. Of course he does, for he feels that he has to quiet his conscience and keep up his good repute. But does he care for the glory of God? By no means. If he did he would give more than money. His heart's prayers would go up for the progress of the kingdom. Does he sigh and cry because of the sins of the times? Do you find him alone with God pouring out his heart in anguish because even in his own family there are those who are not converted to God? Did you ever see in him a high and holy joy when sinners are converted—an exultation because the kingdom of Christ is coming? Oh no, he never rises to that. All the service of God is outward to him. He has never entered into the core and heart of spiritual things, and he never can.

*"The carnal mind,"* even when it is religious, is still *"enmity against God"* (Rom. 8:7). It is not reconciled to God, neither indeed can it be. There must be a spiritual mind created in the man. He must become a new creature in Christ Jesus before he can appreciate, understand, and enjoy spiritual things.

Let us come back to where we started: *"Ye must be born again"* (John 3:7). We must be born of the Spirit; we must receive a supernatural life by being quickened from our death in sin. We cannot bear the fruit of the Spirit until we have the inner life of the Spirit. Ishmael will be Ishmael, and Isaac will be Isaac. As the man is, such will his conduct be. The man of sight and reason and human power may do his best as Ishmael did, but only the child of the promise will rise to the life and walk of faith as Isaac did.

"Hard lines," you may say. Sometimes it is a great blessing to have those hard lines drawn and drawn very straight, too. By this means we may be set on the right track for eternity. Someone said the other day to a friend of mine, "I once went to hear Mr. Spurgeon, and when I went into the Tabernacle, if you had asked me about myself, I would have judged that I was as religious a man as ever lived in Newington, and as good a man, certainly, as ever made part of a congregation. All this was reversed when I heard the Gospel that day. I came out of the place with every feather plucked out of me. I felt myself the most wretched sinner that could be on the face of the earth, and I said I will never go to hear that man again, for he has spoiled me altogether.

"Yes," he said, "but that was the best thing that could have happened to me. I was made to look away from myself, and all that I could do, to God and to His omnipotent grace, and to understand that I must pass under my Creator's hand again, or I could never see His face with joy."

I hope you know this truth for yourself, a solemn truth it is. Even as first of all God made Adam, so must He make us over again, or else we can never bear His image or behold His glory. We must come under the influence of the promise and live upon the promise, or our lives will never be guided by right principles or directed to right ends.

# CHAPTER FOUR

# DIFFERING HOPES

## ≈ 4 ≈

# DIFFERING HOPES

*And as for Ishmael, I have heard thee: Behold,*
*I have blessed him, and will make him fruitful,*
*and will multiply him exceedingly; twelve princes*
*shall he beget, and I will make him a great nation.*
*But my covenant will I establish with Isaac,*
*which Sarah shall bear unto thee at this*
*set time in the next year.*
—Genesis 17:20–21

I t is not at all strange that two people, as different in their birth and nature as Ishmael and Isaac were, became very different in their hopes. To Isaac, the covenant promise became the polestar of his being. For Ishmael, no such light had arisen. Ishmael aimed at large things, for he was the natural son of one of the greatest of men. Isaac looked for still higher objects because he was the child of the promise and the inheritor of the covenant of grace that the Lord had made with Abraham.

Ishmael, with his high and daring spirit, looked to found a nation that would never be subdued, a race as untamable as the wild ass of the desert. His desire has been abundantly granted. The Bedouin Arabs are to this day true copies of their great ancestor. Ishmael in life and death realized the narrow, earthly hopes for which he looked. But in the book of those who saw the day of Christ, and died in hope of the glory, his name is not entered. Isaac, on the other hand, saw far ahead, even to the day of Christ. *"For he looked for a city which hath foundations, whose builder and maker is God"* (Heb. 11:10).

Ishmael, like Passion in *Pilgrim's Progress,* had his best things here on earth. Isaac, like Patience, waited for his best things to come in the future. His treasures were not in the tent and in the field but in things not yet seen. He had received the great covenant promise, and there he found greater riches than all the flocks of Nebaioth, the firstborn of Ishmael, could minister to him. Upon his eye the daystar of promise had shone, and he expected a full noon of blessing in the fullness of the appointed time. The promise was so strong upon him that it directed the current of his thoughts and expectations. Is it so with you, my reader? Have you received and embraced the promise of eternal life? Are you, therefore, hoping for things not seen as yet? Have you an eye to that which none can behold except believers in the faithfulness of God? Have you left the rut of present sensual perception for the way of faith in the unseen and eternal?

No doubt the reception of the promise and the enjoyment of its hopes influenced the mind and temper of Isaac so that he was of a restful spirit. For him there were no wars and fightings. He yielded the present and waited for the future. Isaac felt that because he was born after the promise it was for God to bless him and to fulfill the promise that He had made concerning him. He, therefore, remained with Abraham and kept himself aloof from the outside world. He both quietly hoped and patiently waited for the blessing of God. His eye was on the future, on the great nation yet to come, the Promised Land, and on the yet more glorious promised Seed in whom all the nations of the earth would be blessed. For all this he looked to God alone, wisely judging that He who gave the promise would Himself see to its fulfillment.

Isaac, although he was active, manifested none of the proud self-reliance that was so apparent in Ishmael. He was energetic in his own way, with a calm confidence in God and a quiet submission to His supreme will. Year after year he held on in the separated life and braved unarmed the danger that arose from his heathen neighbors—dangers that Ishmael confronted with his sword and with his bow. His trust was in the voice that said, *"Touch not mine anointed, and do my prophets no harm"* (1 Chron. 16:22). He was a man of peace, and yet he lived as securely as his warlike brother. His faith in the promise gave him hope of security, yes, gave him security itself, though the Canaanite was still in the land.

The promise operates upon our present life by creating in us an elevation of spirit, a life above visible surroundings, a calm and heavenly frame of mind. Isaac finds his bow and his spear in his God; Jehovah is his shield and his exceeding great reward. Without a foot of land to call his own, Isaac dwelled as a sojourner and a stranger in the land that God had given him by promise. He was content to live upon the promise and count himself rich in joys to come. He had a remarkably quiet and steady spirit for a man leading the strange unearthly life of one of the great pilgrim fathers. This spirit sprang out of his simple faith in the promise of the unchanging God.

Hope, kindled by a divine promise, affects the entire life of a man in his inmost thoughts, ways, and feelings. It may seem to be of less importance than correct moral deportment. Actually it is of vital significance, not only in itself, but in that which it produces upon the mind, heart, and life. The secret hope of a man is a truer test of his condition before God than the acts of any one day or even the public devotions of a year. Isaac pursued his quiet holy way until he grew old and blind and gently fell asleep trusting in his God: his God who had revealed Himself to him and had called him to be His friend. God had said, *"Sojourn in this land, and I will be with thee, and will bless thee"* (Gen. 26:3), and *"in thy seed shall all the nations of the earth be blessed"* (v. 4).

As a man's hopes are, such is he. If his hope is in the promise of God, it is, it must be, well with him.

Reader, what are your hopes? "Why," says one, "I am waiting until a relative dies, and then I will be rich. I have great expectations." Another hopes in his steadily growing trade. A third expects much from a promising speculation. Hopes that can be realized in a dying world are mere mockeries. Hopes that have no outlook beyond the grave are dim windows for a soul to look through. Happy is he who believes the promise and feels assured of its fulfillment to himself in due time. He leaves all else in the hands of infinite wisdom and love. Such hope will endure trials, conquer temptations, and enjoy heaven below.

When Christ died on the cross, our hopes began; when He rose, they were confirmed. When He went up on high, they began to be fulfilled; when He comes a second time, they will be realized. In this world we will have pilgrim's fare and a table spread in the presence of our enemies. In the world to come we will possess the land that flows with milk and honey, a land of peace and joy, where the sun will no more go down, neither will the moon withdraw herself. (See Isaiah 60:20.) Until then we hope, and our hope is based on the promise.

# CHAPTER FIVE

# PERSECUTION

## ❧ 5 ❧

# PERSECUTION

*Now we, brethren, as Isaac was, are the children of
promise. But as then he that was born after the flesh
persecuted him that was born after the Spirit,
even so it is now.*
—Galatians 4:28–29

When brothers differ as greatly as Ishmael
and Isaac, it is not surprising if they fall
out and indulge unkind feelings. Ishmael
was older than Isaac, and when the time came for
Isaac to be weaned, his mother, Sarah, saw the son
of the bondwoman mocking her child. So early had
the difference of birth and condition begun to display itself. This may serve us as an indication of
what we may expect if we possess the God-given
life and are heirs according to the promise. Those
who are under the bondage of the law cannot love
those who are freeborn by the Gospel, and in some
way or another they soon display their enmity.

We are not now thinking of the hostility between the wicked world and the church but of that which exists between men of a merely natural religion and those who are born of God. We speak not of the Philistines opposing Isaac but of his brother Ishmael mocking him. Keenest of all is this opposition of the externally religious to those who are born from above and worship God in spirit and in truth. Many precious children of God have suffered bitterly from the cruel hatred of those who professed to be their friends.

Probably the motive of Ishmael was envy. He could not endure that the little one should have preeminence over himself. He seemed to say, "This is the heir, and therefore I hate him." Perhaps he mocked Isaac's heirship and boasted that he had as good a right to the estate as the child of the promise could ever have. Thus do those who merely profess religion envy the condition of believers and reckon themselves to be quite as good as the best of those who hope to be saved by the grace of God. They do not desire the grace of God themselves, and yet, like the dog in the manger, they cannot bear that others should have it. They envy the saints their hope, their peace of mind, and their enjoyment of the favor of God. If any of you find this to be true, do not be in the least surprised.

The envy of Ishmael displayed itself most at the great feast that had been made at his brother's weaning. And formalists, like the elder brother in the parable, do become most provoked when there is most occasion for rejoicing in connection with the

Father's beloved child. The music and dancing of the true family are gall and wormwood to proud, base-born brothers. When full assurance is weaned from doubt and holy delight is weaned from the world, then the carnal religionist puts on a sneer. He calls the godly mad or fanatical, or he murmurs with sullen sarcasm, "Poor fools! Let them alone; they are a sadly deluded crew." People who are religious but not truly regenerated, who are working and hoping to be saved by their own merits, usually exhibit a bitter hatred toward those who are born of the promise.

Sometimes they mock their feebleness. Maybe Ishmael called Isaac a mere baby, just weaned. So are believers a feeble folk and exceedingly likely to excite the derision of those who think themselves strong-minded. Isaac could not deny that he was weak. Neither can believers deny that they are faulty and are subject to infirmities that may put them under just censure. The world makes more of this than justice will allow and mocks at saints for weaknesses that in others would be overlooked. We must not think it a strange thing if our insignificance and imperfection should set proud and self-righteous Pharisees jeering at us and our Gospel.

Frequently the sport is raised by the believer's pretensions. Isaac was called "the heir," and Ishmael could not bear to hear it. "Look," says the legalist, "yonder man was not long ago a known sinner; now he says he has believed in Jesus Christ, and therefore he declares that he knows himself to be saved and accepted and sure of heaven. Did you ever hear of such presumption?" He who hugs his chains hates the presence of a free man. He who refuses the mercy of God because he proudly trusts his own merits is angry with the man who rejoices to be saved by grace.

Perhaps the little Isaac, the child of such aged parents, seemed odd and strange to the young half-bred Egyptian. No person is as much a foreigner to his fellowmen as a man born from above. To live by faith upon the promise of God ought to seem the most proper and natural thing in the world, but it is not so esteemed. On the contrary, men count those who believe in God and act upon such a belief to be strange beings. Wretched boys in the streets still hoot at foreigners, and men of the world still jest at true believers because of their unworldly spirit and conduct. To us this is a testimony for good, for our Lord said, *"If ye were of the world, the world would love his own: but because ye are not of the world, but I have chosen you out of the world, therefore the world hateth you"* (John 15:19).

In a thousand ways, many of them too petty to be worthy of mention, the believer can be made to bear *"trial*[s] *of cruel mockings"* (Heb. 11:36), and he ought to be prepared to do so. After all, it is but a small matter to be persecuted nowadays. The fires of Smithfield are quenched, the Lollards' tower contains no prisoners, and not even a thumbscrew remains in use. Courage, good brother! Even if you are ridiculed, no bones will be broken. If you are brave enough to despise contempt, even your sleep will not be disturbed.

Ishmael's mocking Isaac is only one among ten thousand proofs of the enmity that exists between the seed of the woman and the seed of the serpent. The mixture of these two in Abraham's household came about through his going down into Egypt and acting in an unbelieving manner toward Pharaoh. Then the Egyptian bondwoman was given to Sarah, and the evil element came into the camp. Sarah, in an evil hour, gave the bondwoman to her husband, hence ten thousand tears.

No association of the unregenerate with the church of God will avail to alter their nature. An Ishmael in Abraham's encampment is Ishmael still. Today, the fiercest enemies of the truth of God are the aliens in our communion. They are those who make believers in sound evangelical teaching look like strangers in the churches that were founded on the basis of scriptural doctrine. They make us foreigners in our own land. They are lenient to all manner of heresy. Yet they sneer at the believer in the doctrines of grace as old-fashioned and big-oted—a belated mortal who ought studiously to seek out a grave and bury himself. The man who trusts his God and believes in His covenant will be able to survive all mockeries. He will count the reproach of Christ greater riches than all the treasures of Egypt.

It is by no means shameful to trust God. On the contrary, it is a point of honor with good men to trust in Him who is faithful and true. If they have to suffer for it, they do so joyfully. Gird yourselves, therefore, with a holy courage, you who are learning through grace to live upon the promise of God by faith. Was not the great Head of the family despised and rejected by men? Must not the rest of the brotherhood be conformed to the Firstborn? If we are made partakers of Christ's sufferings, we will be partakers of His glory. Let us take part and lot with the crucified Heir of all things.

# CHAPTER SIX

# THE PARTING

## ❧ 6 ❧

# THE PARTING

*Nevertheless what saith the scripture? Cast out the bondwoman and her son: for the son of the bondwoman shall not be heir with the son of the freewoman.*
—Galatians 4:30

I saac and Ishmael lived together for a time. The self-religionist and the believer in the promise may be members of the same church for years, but they are not agreed and cannot be happy together. Their principles are essentially opposed. As the believer grows in grace and enters upon his spiritual manhood, he will be more and more disagreeable to the legalist. It will ultimately be seen that the two have no fellowship with one another. They must separate, and this is the word that will be fulfilled to the Ishmaelite: *"Cast out this bondwoman and her son: for the son of this bondwoman shall not be heir with my son, even with Isaac"* (Gen. 21:10). Grievous as the parting may be, it will be according to the divine will and according to the necessities of the case. Oil and water will not mingle, neither will the natural man's religion agree with that which is born of the promise and sustained by the promise. Their parting will be only the outward result of a serious difference that always existed.

Ishmael was sent away, but he soon ceased to regret it. He found greater freedom with the wild tribes of the country, among whom he soon became a great man. He prospered much and became the father of princes. He was in his proper sphere in the wide world. There he had honor and gained a name among its great ones. It often happens that the carnally religious man has many excellent habits and ways about him. Having a desire to shine, he goes into society and is appreciated and becomes notable. The world is sure to love its own.

The aspiring religionist usually forsakes his first friends and openly declares, "I have given up the old-fashioned style of religion. The saints were all very well while I was poor, but now I have made a fortune and I feel that I must mix with a more fashionable set of people." He does so, and he has his reward. Ishmael had his portion in this life and never expressed a desire to share in the heavenly covenant and its mysterious blessings. If you would feel freer and more at home in society than in the church of God, you can know assuredly that you belong to the world. Do not deceive yourself. As your heart is, such are you. No measure of force can turn Ishmael into Isaac or a worldling into an heir of heaven.

Outwardly, and in this present life, the heir of the promise did not appear to have the best of it.

Nor, indeed, should this be expected, since those who choose their heritage in the future have, in fact, agreed to accept trial in the present.

Isaac experienced certain afflictions that Ishmael never knew. He was mocked, and he was at last laid on the altar. Nothing of the sort happened to Ishmael. You, who like Isaac are the children of the promise, must not envy those who are the heirs of this present life, though their lot seems easier than your own. Your temptation is to do so, just like the psalmist did when he was grieved because of the prosperity of the wicked. There is in this fretting a measure of running back from our spiritual choice. Have we not agreed to take our part in the future rather than in the present? Do we rue the bargain? Moreover, how absurd it is to envy those who are themselves so much to be pitied! To lose the promise is practically to lose everything, and the self-righteous have lost it.

These worldly ones who profess religion have no spiritual light or life, and they desire none. What a loss, to be in the dark and not to know it! They have enough religion to make them respectable among men and comfortable in their own consciences. However, this is a sorry gain if they are abominable in the sight of God. They feel no inward fightings and wrestlings. They find no contention of the old man against the new. So they go through life with a jaunty air, knowing nothing until their end comes. What wretchedness to be so befuddled! Again, I say, do not envy them. Far better is the life of Isaac with its sacrifice than that of Ishmael with its sovereignty and wild freedom. For all the world-ling's greatness will soon be ended and leave nothing behind it but that which will make the eternal world to be the more miserable.

Yet do not dream that believers are unhappy. If in this life alone we had hope, we would be miserable indeed. The promise lights up our whole career and makes us truly blessed. God's smile beheld by faith gives us fullness of joy. Put the believer's life at the greatest possible disadvantage, paint it in the darkest colors, take away from it not only comforts but also necessities, and even then the Christian at his worst is better than the worldling at his best. Let Ishmael have the whole world. Yes, give him as many worlds as there are stars in the midnight sky, and we will not envy him. It is still our obligation to take up our cross and to be strangers and foreigners with God in this land, as all our fathers were.

The promise, though it seems far off to others, we do, by faith, realize and embrace, and in it we find a heaven below. Abiding with God and with His people, we count our lot far better than that of the greatest and most honored of the children of this world. The prospect of our Lord's second coming, and of our own eternal glory in fellowship with Him, suffices to fill us with contentment while we wait for His appearing.

This difference on earth will lead to a sad division in death. The child of the bondwoman must be cast out in eternity as well as in time. None who claim it by their own doings or boast that they have won it by their own strength can enter heaven. Glory is reserved for those who are saved by grace, and none who trust in self can enter there. What a terrible thing it will be when those who labored to establish their own righteousness, and would not submit to the righteousness of Christ, will be driven out! How they will then envy those lowly ones who were pleased to accept pardon through the blood of Jesus! How they will discover their folly and wickedness in having despised the gift of God by preferring their own righteousness to that of the Son of God!

As the people who are represented by Ishmael and Isaac are ultimately parted, so the principles upon which they rest must never be mingled, for they can by no means be made to agree. We cannot be saved in part by self and in part by the promise of God. The principle and notion of earning salvation must be expelled from the mind. Every degree and form of it must be cast out. If we are so unwise as to place our dependence partly on grace and partly on merit, we will be resting one foot on a rock and the other on the sea. Our fall will be certain. There can be no dividing of the work or of the glory of salvation. It must be all of grace or all of works, all of God or all of man. It cannot be half of one and half of the other. Cease from the vain attempt to unite two principles that are as adverse as fire and water.

The promise, and the promise alone, must be the foundation of our hope, and all notions of righteousness by works must be sternly dismissed as irreconcilable with salvation by grace. We must not begin in the spirit and hope to be made perfect in the flesh. Our religion must be alike. To sow with mingled seed or to wear a garment of linen and wool mixed was forbidden to the Lord's ancient people. For us it is unlawful to mingle mercy and merit, grace and debt. Whenever the notion of salvation by merit or feeling or ceremonies comes in, we must cast it out without delay, though it be as dear to us as Ishmael was to Abraham. Faith is not sight; the spirit is not the flesh; grace is not merit; and we must never forget the distinction, lest we fall into grievous error and miss the heritage that belongs only to the heirs according to promise.

Here is our confession of faith:

> *Knowing that a man is not justified by the works of the law, but by the faith of Jesus Christ, even we have believed in Jesus Christ, that we might be justified by the faith of Christ, and not by the works of the law: for by the works of the law shall no flesh be justified.* (Gal. 2:16)

Here also is the clear line of distinction as to the method of our salvation, and we desire to keep it plain and obvious:

> *Even so then at this present time also there is a remnant according to the election of grace. And if by grace, then is it no more of works: otherwise grace is no more grace. But if it be of works, then is it no more grace: otherwise work is no more work.* (Rom. 11:5–6)

Reader, do you see this?

# CHAPTER SEVEN

# WHOSE ARE THE PROMISES?

## ≈ 7 ≈

# WHOSE ARE THE PROMISES?

*He that believeth on the Son hath everlasting life.*
—John 3:36

The Lord is ever just and good toward His creatures. It is His nature to be so. But there was no necessity either in His justice or in His goodness that He should make promises of grace to those who had rebelled against Him. Man has forfeited every form of claim upon his Maker that he may have thought he had. He has broken the pure and holy law that he was under bond to have obeyed. Nothing is now due to man but the reward of his sins. If God would now deal with man upon the ground of strict justice, He must condemn and punish him. Anything in the way of a favor to a guilty creature must proceed only from the undeserved mercy and sovereign goodness of God. It must spring spontaneously from the goodwill and pleasure of the Most High. The promises of grace flow from the boundless love of God and from that alone. They could not have proceeded from any other source. No single one of the race of man has any natural right to promises of blessing, nor can the whole world of men deserve them. God has made promises to men out of His own free will and good pleasure from no motive except for the love that lies within Himself.

He has chosen to make His promises to the elect persons, who in the process of time are discovered by their exercising faith in Him. Those whom God has chosen are led by the Holy Spirit to choose God and His way of salvation by faith in Christ Jesus. Those of the elect who come to years of searching are led to faith in Jesus. All who have faith in Him may conclude beyond doubt that they are of the chosen number to whom the promises are given.

To those who live and die in unbelief there is no absolute and personal promise of God. They are not under grace but under law, and to them belong the threatenings and not the promises. They prefer another method of dealing with life than that of the gracious promise, and in the end they perish as the result of their foolish preference. The chosen of the Lord are led to relinquish the proud way of self and merit. They take to the road of faith and so find rest unto their souls. To believe the Word of God and to trust in Him whom God has sent to be our Savior may seem like a small thing, but indeed it is not so. It is the sign of election, the token of regeneration, the mark of coming glory. So to believe that God is true so much that one rests his eternal interests upon His promise shows a heart reconciled to God, a spirit in which the seed of perfect holiness is present.

When we believe God as He is revealed in Christ Jesus, we believe all His promises. Confidence in the person involves confidence in all that he speaks. Therefore, we accept all the promises of God as being sure and certain. We do not trust one promise and doubt another, but we rely upon each one as true. We believe each promise to be true to us regardless of our condition and circumstances. We argue from general statements to particular applications. He who has said that He will save those who believe in Him will save me since I believe in Him. Every blessing that He has engaged to bestow upon believers He will bestow upon me as a believer. This is sound reasoning, and by it we justify the faith by which we live and are comforted. Not because I deserve anything, but because God has freely promised it to me in Christ Jesus; therefore, I will receive it. This is the reason and ground of our hope.

One wonders at first sight why not all men believe in God. It would seem as if this mark of divine election would be universally present. One must remember that God cannot lie, and there is no reason to suspect Him of change or failure of ability to keep His word. Yet so false is the heart of man that he doubts his Maker. He hates his God and therefore disbelieves Him. It is the surest proof of man's natural enmity against God that he dares to impute falsehood to One who is truth itself. *"He that believeth not God hath made him a liar; because he believeth not the record that God gave of his Son"* (1 John 5:10).

Real, practical trust in the living God, easy as it seems to be, is a virtue that was never practiced by an unrenewed heart. The glorious atonement made by the incarnate Son of God is worthy of the reliance of all mankind. One would have imagined that every sinner would have washed at once in this cleansing fountain and without hesitation would have believed in the divine Redeemer. This is very far from being true. Men will not come unto Christ that they may have life. They would rather trust in anything than in the sacrifice of Jesus.

Until the Holy Spirit works a miracle upon a man, he will not confide in the great sacrifice that God has provided and accepted for the putting away of guilt. It so happens that this simple, commonplace matter of faith becomes the distinguishing mark of the chosen of the Lord. No other token is so infallible: *"He that believeth on the Son hath everlasting life"* (John 3:36). Feelings and actions may all serve as evidences. But the master evidence of an interest in the promise of God is faith in Him. *"Abraham believed God, and it was counted unto him for righteousness"* (Rom. 4:3). There were many other good points in the patriarch's character, but this was the decisive one—he believed God. Indeed, this was the root of all else that was commendable in him.

Worldly-wise men despise faith and set it in contrast with virtuous action. This contrast is not fair. One might as well contrast a fountain with its stream or the sun with its own heat. True faith is the mother of holiness, but grace is the mother of faith, so let grace have praise because of her offspring. Do not credit anything but grace for our holiness. Such unfair reasoning comes of wanton malice. If men loved good works as much as they pretend to do, they would love the faith that produces them.

God loves faith because it honors Him and also because it leads to acts of obedience to Him. Obedience to God includes love for our fellowmen. There is more in faith than meets the eye. It is in one aspect the greatest of all good works, even as our Lord Jesus teaches us. The Jews said to Him, *"What shall we do, that we might work the works of God?"* (John 6:28)? They would be willing to perform godlike works, works above all others approved of the Lord. Jesus answered them, *"This is the work of God, that ye believe on him whom he hath sent"* (v. 29). As much as to say—the most divinely approved work possible to you is to believe in the Messiah. To trust in the Lord Jesus is the climax of virtue. Proud men may sneer, but it is true that without faith it is impossible to please God (see Hebrews 11:6), but he who believes in Him is not condemned. (See John 3:18.) The promise is made to him who believes the promise, and to him it will be fulfilled. He who embraces the promise is embraced by the promise. He who accepts Christ is accepted in Christ. He who truly believes is surely saved.

Reader, do you believe your God?

# CHAPTER EIGHT

# A FREE GIFT

## ∽ 8 ∽
# A FREE GIFT

*Even so by the righteousness of one the free gift
came upon all men.*
—Romans 5:18

Observe that word *"gift."* Peter said, *"Whereby
are given unto us exceeding great and precious
promises"* (2 Pet. 1:4). We must credit everything as a gift from God. We live upon divine charity. All that we have we have received as a gift, and
all that we are to have must come in the same way.
*"The wages of sin is death; but the gift of God is eternal
life"* (Rom. 6:23). We are unable to earn anything, but
God is able to give all things. Salvation must be all
a gift, a free gift, an undeserved gift, a spontaneous
gift of divine love. The promise of salvation is of the
same nature.

*"It is more blessed to give than to receive"* (Acts
20:35), and He that is most blessed of all, the ever
blessed God, delights to give. It is as much His

nature to give as it is the nature of the sun to shine or of a river to flow. How blessed we are in being receivers! This is emphasized greatly when we reflect how necessary it is that we should receive. The things we need are such that if we do not obtain them we are lost now and lost forever. We are without life, without light, without hope, and without peace if we are without God. If God does not give to us according to the riches of His grace, we are then worse than naked and poor and miserable. We are utterly and altogether undone. It is not possible that we should deserve such rich gifts. Even if we could deserve anything, it must come to us without money and without price. A promise from God must be a blessing of grace. We cannot say that God should promise us His favor and the priceless blessings that are wrapped up in it.

This teaches us what posture to take up. Pride is not suitable for dependents. He who lives upon gifts should be humble and grateful. We are beggars at the door of mercy. At the Beautiful Gate of the temple we sit down every day to ask for charity, not from the worshippers, but from Him whom angels worship. As often as our Lord passes by, we ask and He gives. We are not surprised that we receive from His love. He has promised to bestow great mercies. He taught us to say, *"Give us this day our daily bread"* (Matt. 6:11), and therefore we are neither ashamed nor afraid to ask all things from Him. Ours is a life of dependence, and we delight to have it so. It is sweet to take all things from the hands of our crucified Lord. Happy is the poverty that leads us to be rich in Christ. We earn nothing, and yet we receive everything, thrice blessed in being hourly partakers of the gift of God. *"Whereby are given unto us exceeding great and precious promises"* (2 Pet. 1:4).

Beloved, this teaching as to the promise coming of pure gift should be exceedingly encouraging to all who know their lost state and admit that they are spiritually bankrupt. To them it is a word of good cheer that everything is freely given to us by God. Why should He not give to them as well as to other needy ones? Those of us who rejoice in God have received all things as free gifts. Why should others not receive the like? They say, "There is nothing freer than a gift." Why should you not receive as well as myself? To one who is willing to give, poverty, on the part of the receiver, is a recommendation instead of an obstacle. Come, then, you who are without merit; Christ will be your merit. Come, you who have no righteousness; He will be your righteousness. Come, you who are as full of sin as an egg is full of food, and the pardoning Lord will put away your sin. Come, you who are utterly forlorn, and be made rich in Jesus. The trade of a beggar will suit you, and you will prosper in it, for I see you have a cruel hunger and an empty wallet.

He who cannot dig should not be ashamed to beg. A beggar needs no stock-in-trade. Old shoes and clouted rags, worn and foul—these form a fit livery for a beggar. Are you not dressed in this fashion spiritually? The poorer the wretch, the more welcome he is at the door of divine charity. The less you have of your own, the more welcome you are to

Him who *"giveth...liberally, and upbraideth not"* (James 1:5).

> Come, ye needy, come and welcome,
> > God's free bounty glorify;
> True belief, and true repentance,
> > Every grace that brings us nigh,
> Without money,
> > Come to Jesus Christ and buy.

Yes, it is all a gift. This is the Gospel that we are sent to preach to you:

> *God so loved the world, that he gave his only begotten Son, that whosoever believeth in him should not perish, but have everlasting life.*　　(John 3:16)

*"This is the record, that God hath given to us eternal life, and this life is in his Son"* (1 John 5:11). On God's part it is all giving. On our part it is all receiving. The promise is already made and made freely. It will be fulfilled and fulfilled freely. God does not begin with giving and then go on to charge a price. No commission is payable upon receipt of His grace. He does not ask for or receive a farthing. His love is altogether a gift. As a gift you may accept His promise. He will not degrade Himself by listening to any other terms.

The word *"gift"* in the text is a plain invitation to the poorest of the poor. Oh, that they would boldly avail themselves of it! The great bell is ringing,

ringing so that all who want to come to the great table of infinite liberality may hear it and draw near. Freely, according to the riches of His grace, God promises salvation and eternal life to all who believe in His Son, Jesus Christ. His promise is firm and sure. Why is it that men do not believe it? Reader, what do you say to this promise so freely given to all believers? Will you believe it and live by it?

# CHAPTER NINE

# THE PROMISE IS A REALITY

# 🗝 9 🗝

# THE PROMISE IS A REALITY

*Whosoever believeth in him [Jesus] should not perish,*
*but have everlasting life.*
—John 3:16

S urely it is a wonderful thing that the eternal
God would make promises to His own creatures. Before He pledged His word, He was
free to do as it pleased Him. After He has made a
promise, His truth and honor bind Him to do as
He has said. To Him, indeed, this is no limiting of
His liberty. The promise is always the declaration of
His sovereign will and good pleasure. It is ever His
delight to act according to His word. It is marvelous
condescension for the free spirit of the Lord to form
for itself covenant bonds. Yet He has done so. The
Lord has made a covenant of grace with men. In it
He has confirmed His promises, not only by pledging His word but by giving His oath:

*That by two immutable things, in which it was impossible for God to lie, we might have a strong consolation, who have fled for refuge to lay hold upon the hope set before us.* (Heb. 6:18)

In that covenant there are many precious promises, all confirmed in Christ Jesus and established forever upon the foundation of divine truthfulness. This is our hope, just as Paul wrote to Titus: *"In hope of eternal life, which God, that cannot lie, promised before the world began"* (Titus 1:2). God has promised, and on the faithfulness of that promise we build our confidence for time and for eternity. We think it no imprudent thing to rest our souls' salvation upon the promise of our faithful Creator. To help us to trust, the promises were not only spoken but written. Men say they like to have an agreement in black and white, and we have that in this case. *"In the volume of the book it is written"* (Ps. 40:7). In the pages of inspiration, the record stands. As we believe our Bibles, we are bound to rely upon the promises contained therein.

It is an area of much weakness in many that they do not treat the promises of God as realities. If a friend makes a promise to them, they regard it as a substantial thing and look for that which it secures. The declarations of God are often viewed as so many words that mean very little. This is most dishonoring to the Lord and very injurious to ourselves. Rest assured that the Lord never trifles with words: *"Hath he said, and shall he not do it?"* (Num. 23:19). His engagements are always kept. David said of the Lord's promises to him, *"Yet he hath made with me an everlasting covenant, ordered in all things, and sure"* (2 Sam. 23:5).

God speaks deliberately, in due order and determination, and we may depend upon it that His words are true. We know that these words will be fulfilled as certainly as they are uttered. Have any who have trusted in the Lord been destroyed? Can an instance be found in which our God has been false to His word? The ages cannot produce a single proof that the promise-making Jehovah has run back from that which He has spoken.

We admire fidelity in men, and we cannot imagine it to be absent from the character of God, and therefore we may safely count on His being as good as His word. It is said of Blücher that, when he was marching to help Wellington at Waterloo, his troops faltered. "It can't be done," they said. "It must be done," was his answer. "I have promised to be there—promised, do you hear? You would not have me break my word." He was at Waterloo for a good purpose, and he would not be hindered, for his promise was given. We praise such faithfulness. We would think little of one who did not exhibit it. Will the Lord God Almighty fail in His promise? No, He will move heaven and earth and shake the universe rather than be behind with His word. He seems to say, "It must be done. I have promised—promised, do you hear?" Before He would fail in His promise, He allowed the death of His own Son. Better Jesus die than the word of the Lord be broken. I say again, depend upon it, the Lord means what He says and will make good every syllable. Yet none but the chosen seed will believe Him. Reader, will you?

God must be true, whoever else may deceive. If all the truth in the whole world could be gathered together, it would be but as a drop in the bucket compared with the truthfulness of God. The veracity of the justest of men is vanity itself compared with the sure truth of God. The faithfulness of the most upright of men is as a vapor, but the faithfulness of God is as a rock. If we trust in good men we ought infinitely more to trust in the good God. Why does it seem an exceptional thing to rest on the promise of God? Somehow it looks to many to be a dreamy, sentimental, mystical business. Yet if we view it calmly it is the most matter-of-fact transaction that can be. God is real. All else is shadowy. He is certain. All else is questionable. He must keep His word; this is an absolute necessity. How else could He be God? To believe in God should be an act of the mind that needs no effort. Even if difficulties could be suggested, the simple and pure in heart would spontaneously say, *"Let God be true, but every man a liar"* (Rom. 3:4). To give God less than an implicit faith is to rob Him of an honor justly due to His spotless holiness.

Our duty to God demands that we accept His promise and act upon it. Every honest man has a right to credence, and much more does the God of truth deserve it. We ought to treat the promise as in itself the substance of the thing promised, just as we look upon a man's check or IOU as an actual payment. Promises to pay are passed from hand to hand in daily business, as if they were the current money of the merchant. God's promises should be regarded in the same light. Let us believe that we have the petitions that we have asked of Him. He wants us to do this and promises to reward such faith.

Let us regard the promise as a thing so sure and certain that we act upon it and allow it to play a chief role in all our calculations. The Lord promises eternal life to those who believe in Jesus. Therefore, if we really believe in Jesus, let us conclude that we have eternal life and rejoice in this great privilege. The promise of God is our best ground of assurance. It is far surer than dreams and visions and fancied revelations, and it is far more to be trusted than feelings, either of joy or sorrow. It is written, *"He that believeth on him is not condemned"* (John 3:18). I believe in Jesus; therefore, I am not condemned. This is good reasoning, and the conclusion is certain. If God has said so, it is so, beyond all doubt. Nothing can be more certain than that which is declared by God Himself. Nothing is surer to happen than that which He has guaranteed by His own hand and seal.

When a soul is under conviction, it perceives the threatenings of the Lord with an intensity of belief that is very noticeable. Its awestricken faith breeds overwhelming terror and dismay within the heart. Why should the promises not be accepted with a similar realization? Why would they not be accepted with the same certainty? If it is made true in the conscience that he who does not believe will be damned, it may be accepted with equal assurance that he who believes and is baptized will be saved. The latter is as much the Word of God as the former.

The tendency of the awakened mind is to dwell upon the dark side of God's Word and feel the full force of it. Then, at the same time we neglect the brighter portion of the record and cast a doubt upon it as though it were too good to be true. This is folly. Every blessing is too good for us to receive if we measure it by our unworthiness. We must remember that no blessing is too good for God to give because of His surpassing excellence. It is after the nature of a God of love to give boundless blessing. If Alexander gave like a king, will Jehovah not give like a God?

We have sometimes heard people say, "As sure as death." We suggest that we might as fitly say, "As sure as life." Gracious things are as sure as *"terrible things in righteousness"* (Ps. 65:5). *"Whosoever believeth in him* [Jesus] *should not perish, but have everlasting life"* (John 3:16). It must be so, for God's Word has said it, and there can be no mistake about it.

Yes, the Lord means what He says. He never mocks men with barren words and empty sounds. Why should He deceive His creatures and ask from them a barren confidence? The Lord may go beyond His Word in giving more than it might be thought to mean. He can never fall short of it. We may interpret His promises upon the most liberal scale. He never fails at rendering true that which we expect because of the promise. Faith never yet outstripped the bounty of the Lord. Let us embrace the promise and rejoice that it is substance and not shadow. Let us even now rejoice in it as being the reality of that for which we are hoping.

# Chapter Ten

# The Treasure of Believers

## ❧ 10 ❧

# THE TREASURE OF BELIEVERS

*It shall be done unto you.*
—John 15:7

God's promises are the special treasure of believers. The substance of faith's heritage lies in them. All the promises of our covenant God are ours to have and to hold as our personal possession. By faith we receive and embrace them, and they constitute our true riches. We have certain most precious things that we can freely enjoy at this present time, but the capital of our wealth, the bulk of our estate lies in the promise of our God. That which we have in hand is only the downpayment of the immeasurable wage of grace that is to be paid to us in due time.

The Lord graciously gives us even now all things necessary for this life and godliness. His choicest blessings are held in reserve for time to come. Grace given to us from day to day is our spending money for traveling expenses on the road home. It is not our estate. Providential supplies are rations on the march but not the ultimate feast of love. We may miss these wayside meals, but we are bound for the Supper of the Lamb. Thieves may rob us of our ready cash, but our special treasure is hidden with Christ in God beyond all fear of loss. The hand that bled to make this treasure ours is keeping it for us.

It is a great joy to have a full assurance of our interest in the promises. We may lose this joyful feeling and we may find it hard to get again, yet the eternal inheritance will still be as truly ours. It is as though a man has in his hand a fair copy of his title deed and much delights himself in reading it until by some mischance his copy is stolen or mislaid. The loss of his writings is not the loss of his rights. His comfortable reading of the title deed is suspended, but his claim to his property is not shaken. The covenant promise is conferred upon every joint-heir with Christ, and there is no such thing as the breaking of this conferment.

Many events may tend to shake the believer's sense of security, but *"the promise...*[is] *sure to all the seed"* (Rom. 4:16). Our greatest possession lies not in any present comfort or confidence that we receive from the promise but in the promise itself. We rely upon the glorious heritage that it secures for us. Our inheritance does not lie on this side of the Jordan. Our city of habitation is not within the borders of the present. We see it from afar, but we wait for its full enjoyment in that illustrious day when our Covenant Head will be revealed in His glory and all His people with Him. God's providence is our earthly pension. God's promise is our heavenly heritage.

Did it ever occur to you to inquire why the way of God's dealing with His chosen would be by promises? He could have bestowed His blessings at once and without giving us notice of His intention. In this way He would have prevented the necessity of a covenant concerning them. There was no necessity in the nature of things for this plan of promising. The Lord might have given us all the mercies we needed without pledging Himself to do so. God, with His great strength of will and firmness of purpose, could have secretly resolved in Himself to do all that He does unto believers without having made them the confidants of His divine counsels. Many a decree has He kept secret from the foundations of the world. Why, then, has He revealed His purposes of blessing? Why is it that His dealings with His people from the gate of Eden until now have been upon the footing of publicly expressed promises?

Does the question not answer itself? In the first place, we could not have been believers if there had not been a promise in which to believe. If the system of salvation is to be by faith, a promise must be made upon which faith can exercise itself. The plan of salvation by faith is selected because it is most suitable to the principle of grace. This involves the giving of promises so that faith may have both food and foundation. Faith without a promise would be a foot without ground to stand upon. Such a faith, if it could be called faith, would be unworthy of the plan of grace. Since faith stands as the great evangelical command, the promise then becomes an essential part of the gospel dispensation.

Moreover, it is a charming thought that our good God purposely gives us promises of good things so that we may enjoy them twice—first by faith, and then by fruition. He gives twice by giving by promise. We also receive twice in embracing the promise by faith. The time for the fulfillment of many promises is not right away. By faith we realize the promise, and the foreshadowing of the expected blessing fills our souls with the benefit long before it actually comes. We have an instance of this upon a large scale in Old Testament saints. The great promise of the Seed in whom the nations would be blessed was the ground of faith, the foundation of hope, and the cause of salvation to thousands of believers before the Son of God actually appeared among men.

Did our Lord not say, *"Abraham rejoiced to see my day: and he saw it, and was glad"* (John 8:56)? The great father of the faithful saw the day of Christ through the telescope of God's promise, by the eye of faith. Abraham did not obtain the fulfillment of that promise, because he fell asleep before the coming of the Lord, as did Isaac and Jacob and many others of the saints. Yet he had Christ to trust in, Christ to rejoice in, and Christ to love and serve. Before He was born in Bethlehem or offered upon Calvary, Jesus was so seen by the faithful that He made them glad. The promise gave them a Savior before the Savior actually appeared. By means of the promise we enter into possession of things not seen as yet. By anticipation we make the coming blessing present to us. Faith obliterates time, annihilates distance, and brings future things at once into its possession.

The Lord has not yet enabled us to join the hallelujahs of heaven. We have not yet passed through the gates of pearl, nor have we trodden the streets of transparent gold. But the promise of such happiness lights up the gloom of our affliction and yields us immediate foretastes of glory. We triumph by faith before our hands actually grasp the palm. We reign with Christ by faith before our heads are encircled with our unfading coronets. Many times we have seen the dawn of heaven while we have beheld light breaking from the promise. When faith has been vigorous, we have climbed where Moses stood and gazed upon the land that flows with milk and honey. When the atheist has declared that there is no Celestial City, we have answered, "Did we not see it from the delectable mountains?" We have seen enough by means of the promise to make us quite sure of the glory that the Lord has prepared for them who love Him. Thus we have obtained our first portion of the promised bliss and found therein a sure pledge of our full and final enjoyment of it.

Do you not think that the promise is also intended to lead us constantly away from the things that are seen, onward and upward to the spiritual and the unseen? The man who lives on the promise of God has risen into quite another atmosphere than that which oppresses us in these low-lying vales of daily life. "It is better," says one, "to trust in the Lord than to put confidence in men. It is better to trust in the Lord than to put confidence in princes." And so, indeed, it is. It is more spiritual, more noble, more inspiring. We need to be raised to this elevated trust by divine power. Our souls naturally cleave unto the dust. Alas, we are hampered by our idolatrous desire to see and touch and handle. We trust our senses but do not have sense enough to trust our God.

The same spirit that led Israel to cry in the wilderness, *"Make us gods to go before us"* (Acts 7:40), leads us to sigh for something tangible by flesh and blood, something upon which our confidence may take hold. We hunger for proofs, tokens, and evidences and will not accept the divine promise as better and surer than all visible signs. Thus we pine away in hungering for tokens and evidences that are visible until we are driven to try the better and surer things that are invisible. Oh, it is a blessed thing for a child of God to be made to leave the sand of things temporal for the rock of things eternal by being called upon to walk by the rule of the promise!

Furthermore, the promises are a help to our hearts toward the realization of the Lord Himself. The child of God, when he believes the promise, is brought to feel that God exists, and that He is the rewarder of those who diligently seek Him. Our tendency is to get away from a real God. We live and move in the region of materialism. We are apt to be enthralled by its influences. We feel these bodies to be real when we have pain in them and this world to be real when we are weighted with its crosses. Yet the body is a poor tent, and the world a mere bubble. These visible things are insubstantial, but they appear sadly solid to us. What we need is to know the invisible to be quite as real as that which is seen and even more so. We need a living God in this dying world, and we must have Him truly near us, or we will fail. The Lord is training His people to perceive Himself. The promise is part of this educational process.

When the Lord gives us faith and we rest on His promise, then we are brought face-to-face with Him. We ask, "Who gave this promise? Who is to fulfill this promise?" and our thoughts are thus led into the presence of the glorious Jehovah. We feel how necessary He is to the whole system of our spiritual life. We realize how truly He enters into it, so that in Him *"we live, and move, and have our being"* (Acts 17:28). If the promise cheers us, it is only because God is behind it. The mere words of the promise are nothing to us unless they come from the lips of God who cannot lie and unless they are brought out by that hand that cannot fail.

The promise is the forecast of the divine purpose, the shadow of the coming blessing. In fact, it is the token of God's own nearness to us. We are cast upon God for the fulfillment of His engagements, and that is one of His reasons for dealing with us by using the method of promise. Perhaps if the Lord had dropped our mercies at our door without a previous hint of their coming, we would not have cared to know from what source they came. If He had sent them with unbroken regularity, even as He makes His sun to rise every morning, we might have slighted them as common results of natural laws. We might have forgotten God because of the punctuality of His providence. Certainly we would have lacked the understanding of the being and loving-kindness of God that we now receive as we read the promise, accept it by faith, plead it in prayer, and in due season see it fulfilled.

That regularity of divine bounty that ought to sustain and increase faith is often the means of weakening it. He whose bread comes to him by a government annuity or a quarterly rent is tempted to forget that God has any hand in it. It ought not to be so. Through the hardness of our hearts, such an ill result does frequently follow from the constancy of a gracious providence.

I should not wonder if those Israelites who were born in the wilderness and had gathered manna every morning for years had also ceased to wonder at it or to see the hand of the Lord in it. Shameful stupidity! But, ah, how common! Many a person has lived from hand to mouth and seen the hand of the Lord in the gift of every morsel of bread. At last by God's goodness he has prospered in this world and obtained a regular income. This income he has received without care and trouble, and shortly he has come to look at it as the natural result of his own industry. No longer does he praise the loving-kindness of the Lord. To be living without the conscious presence of the Lord is a horrible state of affairs. Supplied, but not by God! Sustained without the hand of God! It is better to be poor or sick or exiled and thus to be driven to approach our heavenly Father.

To avoid our coming under the curse of forgetting God, the Lord is pleased to put His choicest blessings into connection with His own promises and to call forth our faith in reference to them. He will not allow His mercies to become veils to hide His face from the eyes of our love. He makes them windows through which He looks upon us. The Promiser is seen in the promise, and we watch to see His hand in the performance. Therefore, we are saved from that natural atheism that lurks within the heart of man.

I think it well to repeat that we are put under the regime of promise in order that we may grow in faith. How could there be faith without a promise? How can we be growing in faith without grasping more and more of the promise? We are made to remember in the hour of need that God has said, *"Call upon me in the day of trouble: I will deliver thee"* (Ps. 50:15). One who has faith believes this word, calls upon God, and finds himself delivered. Thus he is strengthened and made to glorify the Lord.

Sometimes faith does not find the promise fulfilled at the moment and has to wait a while. This is fine exercise for her and serves to test her sincerity and force. This test brings assurance to the believer and fills him with comfort. By and by the answer is given to prayer, the promised blessing is bestowed, faith is crowned with victory, and glory is given to God. Meanwhile, the delay has produced the patience of hope and made every mercy to wear a double value. Promises act as a training ground for faith. They are poles and leaping-bars for the athletic exercise of our young faith. By the use of promises, faith grows to be so strong that it can break through a troop or leap over a wall. When our confidence in God is firm we laugh at impossibility and cry, *"It shall be done"* (John 15:7), but this could not be if there were not an infallible promise in which faith could gird itself.

Those promises that as yet are unfulfilled are precious helps to our advance in the spiritual life. We are encouraged by exceeding great and precious promises to aspire to higher things. The prospect of good things to come strengthens us to endure and to press forward. You and I are like little children who are learning to walk and are induced to take step after step with an apple being held out to them. We are persuaded to try the trembling legs of our faith by the sight of a promise. Thus we are drawn to go a step nearer to our God. The little one is very apt to cling to a chair; it is hard to get him to let go and venture upon his feet. At last he becomes daring enough for a tiny trip, which he ends at his mother's knees. This little venture leads to another and another until he runs alone. The apple plays a great part in the training of the babe, and so does the promise in the education of faith. Promise after promise we have received. I trust that we can give up crawling on the earth and clinging to the things that rest upon it, and we can commit ourselves to the walk of faith.

The promise is a necessary instrument in the education of our souls in all manner of spiritual graces and actions. How often have I said, "My Lord, I have received much from You; blessed be Your name for it. However, there is still a promise that I have not enjoyed. Therefore, I will go forward until I attain its fulfillment! The future is an unknown country, but I enter it with Your promise, and expect to find in it the same goodness and mercy that have followed me so far. Yes, I look for greater things than these."

Nor must I forget to remind you that the promise is part of the economy of our spiritual condition here below because it excites prayer. What is prayer but the promise pleaded? A promise is, so to speak, the raw material of prayer. Prayer irrigates the fields of life with the waters that are stored up in the reservoirs of promise. The promise is the power of prayer. We go to God, and we say to Him, "Do as You have said. O Lord, here is Your Word; we ask You to fulfill it." Thus the promise is the bow by which we shoot the arrows of supplication.

In my time of trouble, I like to find a promise that exactly fits my need and then to put my finger on it and say, "Lord, this is Your Word. I ask You to prove that it is so, by carrying it out in my case. I believe that this is Your own writing, and I pray that You make it good to my faith." I believe in absolute inspiration, and I humbly look to the Lord for absolute fulfillment of every sentence that He has put on record. I delight to hold the Lord to the very words that He has used and to expect Him to do as He has said because He has said it. It is a great thing to be driven to prayer by necessity. It is a better thing to be drawn to it by the expectation that the promise stimulates. Would we pray at all if God did not find us an occasion for praying and then encourage us with gracious promises of an answer? As it is, in the order of providence we are tried, and then we try the promises. We are brought to spiritual hunger, and then we are fed on the Word that proceeds out of the mouth of God. (See Matthew 4:4.)

By the system that the Lord follows with His chosen, we are kept in constant communication with Him and are not allowed to forget our heavenly Father. We are often at the throne of grace, blessing God for promises fulfilled, and pleading promises on which we rely. We pay innumerable visits to the divine dwelling place because there is a promise to plead and a God waiting to be gracious. Is this not an order of things for which to be grateful? Should we not magnify the Lord because He does not pour upon us showers of unpromised blessings? He actually enhances the value of His benefits by making them the subjects of His promises and the objects of our faith.

# CHAPTER ELEVEN

# EXCEEDING ALL EXPECTATION

## ≈ 11 ≈

# EXCEEDING ALL EXPECTATION

*Whereby are given unto us exceeding great
and precious promises.*
—2 Peter 1:4

We have thought upon the promises as our treasure. It is time that we take a survey of them and calculate their value. Since the promises are our estate, let us form a correct estimate of our wealth. We may not fully know how rich we are. It will be a pity to pine in poverty from ignorance of our large property. May the Holy Spirit help us to form a just appraisal of the riches of grace and glory reserved for us in the covenant of promise!

The apostle Peter spoke of the promises as *"exceeding great and precious."* They do indeed exceed all things with which they can be compared. None ever promised as God has done. Kings have promised even to the half of their kingdoms. But what of that? God promised to give His own Son, and even His own Self, to His people, and He did it. Princes draw a line somewhere, but the Lord sets no bounds to the gifts that He ordains for His chosen.

The promises of God not only exceed all precedent, but they also exceed all imitation. Even with God Himself for an example, none have been able to vie with Him in the language of liberality. The promises of Jehovah are as much above all other promises as the heavens are above the earth.

They also exceed all expectation. He does for us *"exceeding abundantly above all that we ask or think"* (Eph. 3:20). Nobody could have imagined that the Lord would have made such promises as He has made. They surpass the dreams of romance. Even the most sanguine hopes are left far behind, and the loftiest conceptions are outdone. The Bible must be true, for it could not have been invented. The promises contained in it are greater for quantity and better for quality than the most expectant individual could have looked for. God surprises us with the surpassing fullness of His cheering words. He overwhelms us with favors until, like David, we sit down in wonder and cry, "Why do I receive so much that I do not deserve?"

The promises exceed all measurement. There is an abyss of depth in them as to meaning, a heaven of height in them as to excellence, and an ocean of breadth in them as to duration. We might say of every promise, "It is high. I cannot attain it." As a whole, the promises exhibit the fullness and all-sufficiency of God. Like God Himself, they fill all things. Unbounded in their range, they are everywhere about us, whether we wake or sleep, go forth or return. They cover the whole of life from the cradle to the tomb. A sort of omnipresence may be ascribed to them. They surround us in all places and at all times. They are our pillow when we fall asleep, and when we awake they are still with us. *"How precious also are thy thoughts unto me, O God! how great is the sum of them!"* (Ps. 139:17). They exceed all conception and calculation. We admire them and adore their Giver, but we can never measure them.

The promises even exceed all experience. Those men of God who have known the Lord for fifty or sixty years have never yet extracted the whole of the marrow from His promise. Still it might be said, "The arrow is beyond thee." (See 1 Samuel 20:37.) Something better and deeper yet remains to be searched out in the future. He who dives deepest by experience into the depths of the divine promises is fully aware that there is yet a lower depth of grace and love unfathomable. The promise is longer than life, broader than sin, deeper than the grave, and higher than the clouds. He who is most acquainted with the golden book of promise is still a new beginner in its study. Even the ancients of Israel find that this volume passes knowledge.

Certainly I need not say that the promises exceed all expression. If all the tongues of men and of angels were given to me, I could not tell you how great the promises of God are. They exceed not only one language, but all languages. They surpass the glowing praises of all the enthusiasts that have ever spoken. Even angels before the throne still desire to look into these marvels, for they cannot yet reach the mystery—the length, breadth, and height. In Christ Jesus everything exceeds description. The promises in Him exhaust the force of all speech, human or divine. It is vain for me to attempt the impossible.

Peter said the promises are exceedingly *"great,"* and he said so correctly. They come from a great God, they assure us of great love, they come to great sinners, they work great results for us, and they deal with great matters. They are as great as greatness itself. They bring us the great God to be our God forever and ever. God's first promise was that in which He engaged to give us His Son. We want to say, *"Thanks be unto God for his unspeakable gift"* (2 Cor. 9:15), but do not let the words glide too easily over the tongue. For God to give His only begotten Son is beyond all conception a great deed of love. Indeed, *"great"* seems too little a word to describe such a miracle of love.

When the Lord had given His Son, freely delivering Him up for us all—what happened then? He promised to give the Holy Spirit, the Comforter, to abide with us forever. Can we measure the value of that great promise? The Holy Spirit came down at Pentecost in fulfillment of that ancient prophecy. Was not that marvelous descent an exceedingly great and precious gift? Remember that the Holy Spirit works in us all those graces that prepare us for the society of heaven. Glory be to God for this visitation of boundless grace!

What next? Our Lord has given us now the promise that He will come again without a sin offering unto salvation. Can all the saints put together fully measure the greatness of the promise of the Second Advent? This means infinite happiness for saints. What else has He promised? Why, that because He lives we will live also. We will possess an immortality of bliss for our souls. We will also enjoy a resurrection for our bodies. We will reign with Christ. We will be glorified at His right hand. Promises fulfilled and promises unfulfilled, promises for time and promises for eternity—they are indeed so great that it is impossible to conceive of their being greater.

> What more can He say that to you He hath said?
> You who to Jesus for refuge have fled.

O you whose minds are trained to lofty thought, tell me your estimate of the faithful promises! I perceive a promise of the pardon of sin. O you forgiven ones, declare the greatness of this blessing! There is the promise of adoption. Children of God, you begin to know how much love the Father has bestowed upon you with His promises. Shout out your joy! There is the promise of help in every time of need. Tried ones, you know how the Lord sustains and delivers His chosen. Proclaim the largeness of His grace! There is the promise that your strength will fit the needs of your day. You who are working hard for Christ, or bearing His cross from day to day, you feel how exceedingly great that promise is of sure support.

What a word is this: *"No good thing will he with-hold from them that walk uprightly"* (Ps. 84:11)! What a sentence is this: *"All things work together for good to them that love God, to them who are the called accord-ing to his purpose"* (Rom. 8:28). Who can estimate the breadth of such a gracious assurance? No, you need not take that ruler from your pocket. It will not serve you here. If you could take the distance of a fixed star as your base, all reckoning would still be impossible. All the chains that ever measured the acres of the wealthy are useless here. A certain mil-lionaire glories that his estate reaches from sea to sea. No ocean can bound the possessions secured to us by the promise of our faithful God. The theme is so exceedingly great that it exceeds my power of expression, and therefore I hold back.

The verse upon which we are now thinking speaks of *"exceeding great and precious promises."* Greatness and preciousness seldom go together. In this instance they are united in an exceeding degree. When the Lord opens His mouth to make a promise, it is sure to be worthy of Him. He speaks words of exceeding power and richness. Instead of trying to speak of the preciousness of the promises doctrin-ally, I will fall back upon the experience of those who have tried and proved them.

Beloved, how precious the promises are to the poor and needy! Those who know their spiritual poverty discern the value of the promise that meets their case. How precious, also, are the promises to those who have enjoyed the fulfillment of them! We can go back in memory to times and seasons when we were brought low, and the Lord helped us according to His Word. Even before He brought us up out of the horrible pit, we were kept from sinking in the deep mire by looking forward to the time when He would appear for our rescue. His promise kept us from dying of hunger long before we reached the feast of love. In the expectation of future trial our confidence is in the promise. Thus it is very precious to us even before it is actually fulfilled.

The more we believe the promise, the more we find in it to believe. So precious is the Word of the Lord to us that we could part with everything we have rather than throw away a single sentence of it. We cannot tell which promise of the Lord we may next need. That which we have hardly noticed may yet turn out at a certain moment to be essential to our life. Thank God, we are not called to part with any one of the jewels from the breastplate of Holy Scripture. They all are given to us by Christ Jesus to the glory of God!

How precious are the promises when we lie sick, gazing into eternity, sorely tried and tempted through pain and weariness! All depressing circumstances lose their power for evil when our faith takes firm hold upon the promises of God. How sweet to feel I have my head on the promise and my heart on the promise. I rest on the truth of the Most High! Not on earthly vanity, but on heavenly truth, do I repose. There is nothing to be found elsewhere comparable to this perfect rest. The pearl of peace is found among the precious promises. That which can support dying men and cause them to pass into eternity with as much delight as if they were going to a marriage feast is precious indeed. That which lasts forever, and lasts good forever, is most precious. That which brings all things with it and has all things in it is precious indeed. Such is the promise of God.

If such is the greatness and preciousness of the promises, let us joyfully accept and believe them. Will I urge the child of God to do this? No, I will not so dishonor him. Surely he will believe his own Father! Surely, surely, it ought to be the easiest thing in the world for the sons and daughters of the Most High to believe in Him who has given them power to become the children of God! (See John 1:12.) My friends, let us not stagger at the promise through unbelief, but believe up to the hilt!

Furthermore, let us know the promises. Should we not carry them at our fingers' ends? Should we not know them better than anything else? The promises should be the classics of believers. If you have not read the last new book and have not heard the last act of the government, yet you know very well what the Lord God has said, look to see His Word made good. We ought to be so versed in Scripture as to always have at the tip of our tongues the promise that most exactly meets our case. We ought to be transcripts of Scripture. The divine promise should be as much written upon our hearts as upon the pages of the Book.

It is a sad pity that any child of God would be unaware of the existence of the royal promise that would enrich him. It is pitiful for any one of us to be like the poor man who had a fortune left to him about which he knew nothing. Therefore he went on sweeping a crossing and begging for pence. What is the use of having an anchor at home when your ship is in a storm at sea? What avails a promise that you cannot remember so as to plead it in prayer? No matter what else you do not know, be sure you are familiar with those words of the Lord that are more necessary to our souls than bread to our bodies.

Let us also make use of the promises. A little while ago, a friend gave me a check for certain charities, and he said to me, "Be sure that you pay it into the bank today." You may rest assured that this was done. I do not keep checks to look at and play with. They go to the bank, and the cash is received and expended.

The precious promises of our great God are expressly intended to be taken to Him and exchanged for the blessings that they guarantee. Prayer takes the promise to the Bank of Faith and obtains the golden blessing. Mind how you pray. Make real business of it. Let it never be a dead formality. Some people pray a long time but do not get what they are supposed to ask for because they do not plead the promise in a truthful, businesslike way. If you were to go into a bank and stand an hour talking to the clerk and then come out again without your cash, what would be the good of it? If I go to a bank, I pass my check across the counter, take up my money, and go about my business. That is the best way of praying. Ask for what you want, because the Lord has promised it. Believe that you have the blessing, and go forth to your work in full assurance of it. Go from your knees singing because the promise is fulfilled. Thus will your prayer be answered. It is not the length of your prayer, but the strength of your prayer that wins with God. The strength of prayer lies in your faith in the promise that you have pleaded before the Lord.

Last, talk about the promises. Tell the King's household what the King has said. Never keep God's lamps under bushels. Promises are proclamations. Exhibit them on the wall and read them aloud at the market. Oh, that our conversation was more often sweetened with the precious promises of God! After dinner we often sit for half-an-hour and pull our ministers to pieces or scandalize our neighbors. How often is this the Sunday's amusement! It would be far better if we said, "Now, friend, quote a promise," and if the other replied, "And you mention a promise, too." Then let each one speak according to his own personal knowledge concerning the Lord's fulfillment of those promises, and let everyone present tell the story of the Lord's faithfulness to him. By such holy conversation we would warm our own hearts and gladden one another's spirits, and the Sabbath would thus be rightly spent.

Businessmen speak of their trade, travelers of their adventures, and farmers of their crops. Should we not abundantly utter the memory of the Lord's goodness and talk of His faithfulness? If we did so, we would all endorse Peter's statement that our God has given to us *exceeding great and precious promises.*

# CHAPTER TWELVE

# GOD KEEPS HIS WORD TO THE LETTER

## ❧ 12 ❧

# GOD KEEPS HIS WORD
## TO THE LETTER

*And the LORD gave Solomon wisdom,*
*as he promised him.*
—1 Kings 5:12

How the Lord brought about wisdom in Solomon I do not know. But He promised that He would give him wisdom, and He kept His word. The more you think of this, the more remarkable will the fact appear. Solomon was not born under the most hopeful circumstances for wisdom. As the darling child of a somewhat aged father, he was highly likely to be spoiled. As a young man who came to a throne before he was at all fitted for it in the course of nature, he was very likely to have made great blunders and mistakes. As a man of strong animal passions, which in the end overpowered him, he seemed more likely to prove a

profligate than a philosopher. As a person possess-
ing great wealth, unlimited power, and unvarying
prosperity, he had little of that trying experience by
which men acquire wisdom. Who were his teachers?
Who taught him to be wise? His penitent mother
may have set before him much of sound morality
and religion. But she could never have imparted to
him the eminent degree of wisdom that raised him
above all other men and set him upon the pinnacle
of renown. He knew more than others and therefore
could not have borrowed his wisdom from them.
Sages sat at his feet, and his fame brought pilgrims
from the ends of the earth. None could have been
his tutors, since he surpassed them all. How did this
man rise to absolute preeminence in wisdom so as
to make his name throughout all time the synonym
for a wise man?

It is a very mysterious process, this creation of a
master mind. Who will give a young man wisdom?
You can impart knowledge to him but not wisdom.
No tutor, no master, no divine can give another
man wisdom. He has much ado to get a little of
it for himself. Yet God gave Solomon largeness of
heart, as the sands of the sea (see 1 Kings 4:29), and
wisdom unrivaled, for God can do all things. By
operations known only to Himself, the Lord produced in the young king a capacity for observation, reasoning, and prudent action, seldom if ever
equaled. We have often admired the wisdom of
Solomon. I invite you still more to admire the
wisdom of Jehovah by whom Solomon's marvelous
genius was produced.

The reason the Lord brought about this wonder upon Solomon was that He had promised to do it, and He is sure to keep His word. Many other texts would serve to illustrate this as well as this one. The main point that I would like to make is this—that whatever God has promised to anyone, He will surely give it to him. Whether it is wisdom to Solomon or grace to you, my reader, if the Lord has made the promise, He will not allow it to be a dead letter. The God who performed His word in this very remarkable instance, where the matter was so entirely beyond human power and was surrounded with such disadvantageous circumstances, will accomplish His promise in other cases. This fact is true, no matter how difficult and mysterious the process of performance may be.

God will always keep His word to the letter. Actually, He will usually go beyond what the letter seems to mean. In this instance, while He gave Solomon wisdom, He also added to him riches and a thousand other things that did not appear in the compact. *"Seek ye first the kingdom of God, and his righteousness; and all these things shall be added unto you"* (Matt. 6:33). He who makes promises about infinite blessings will throw in everyday things as if they were of small account and were given in as a matter of course, like the grocer's bags in which he packs up our purchases.

From the case of Solomon, and thousands of a similar kind, we learn first that the rule of God's giving is "as He has promised." The page of history sparkles with instances. The Lord promised to our fallen parents that the Seed of the woman would bruise the serpent's head. Behold, that wondrous Seed of the woman has appeared and has gotten for Himself, and for us, the glorious victory of our redemption! In the fulfillment of that one promise we have security for the keeping of all the rest. When God promised to Noah that entering into the ark he would be safe, he found it so. Not one of those innumerable waves that destroyed the antediluvian world could break into his place of safety. When God said to Abraham that He would give him a seed and a land that should be the possession of that seed, it seemed impossible. Still Abraham believed God, and in due time he rejoiced to behold Isaac and to see in him the promised heir.

When the Lord promised Jacob that He would be with him and do him good, He kept His word and gave him the deliverance for which he wrestled at the brook, Jabbok. That long-slumbering promise that the seed of Israel should possess the land that flowed with milk and honey seemed as if it would never be accomplished. It was especially discouraging when the tribes were reduced to slavery in Egypt, and Pharaoh held them with an iron grip and would not let them go. But God, who undertook for His people, brought them out with a high hand and with an outstretched arm on the very day in which He promised to rescue them. He divided the Red Sea also, and He led His people through the wilderness, for He assured them that He would do so. He separated the Jordan in two, and He drove out the Canaanites before His people. He gave Israel the land for their inheritance even as He had promised.

The histories of the Lord's faithfulness are so many that time would fail us to repeat them all. God's words have always in due time been justified by God's acts. God has dealt with men according to His promise. Whenever they have taken hold upon the promise and said, "Do as You have said," God has responded to the plea and proved that it is no vain thing to trust Him. Throughout all time it has been God's unvarying rule to keep His word to the letter and to the moment.

"This is big talk," says one; then we will descend to smaller talk. It is God's way to keep His promise to each individual. We ourselves are living witnesses that God does not forget His word. Tens of thousands of us can testify that we have trusted in Him and have never been brought to ruin. I was once a brokenhearted sinner, cowering down beneath the black cloud of almighty wrath, guilty and self-condemned. I felt that if I were banished forever from Jehovah's presence, I could not say a word against the justice of the sentence. When I read in His Word, *If we confess our sins, he is faithful and just to forgive us our sins*" (1 John 1:9), I went to Him. Tremblingly, I resolved to test His promise. I acknowledged my transgressions unto the Lord, and He forgave the iniquity of my sin. I am telling no idle tale. The deep, restful peace that came to my heart in the moment of forgiveness was so strong that it seemed as if I had begun a new life—as, indeed, I had.

This is how it came about: I heard, one Sabbath day, a poor man speak upon that promise, *"Look unto me, and be ye saved, all ye ends of the earth"* (Isa. 45:22). I could not understand how a mere look to Christ could save me. It seemed too simple an act to effect so great a result. At this point I was ready to try anything; I looked—I looked to Jesus.

It was all I did. It was all I could do. I looked unto Him who is set forth as a propitiation for sin. In a moment I saw that I was reconciled to God. I saw that if Jesus suffered in my stead, I could not suffer, too. If He bore all my sin, I had no more sin to bear. My iniquity must be blotted out if Jesus bore it in my stead and suffered all its penalty. With that thought there came into my spirit a sweet sense of peace with God through Jesus Christ my Lord. The promise was true, and I found it to be so. It happened some thirty-six years ago, but I have never lost the sense of that complete salvation that I then found. Nor have I lost that peace that so sweetly dawned upon my spirit. Since then I have never relied in vain upon a promise of God. I have been placed in positions of great peril, have known great need, have felt sharp pain, and have been weighted with incessant anxieties. Yet the Lord has been true to every line of His word. When I have trusted Him, He has carried me through everything without a failure. I am bound to speak well of Him, and I do so. To this I set my hand and seal, without hesitation or reserve.

The experience of all believers is very similar. We began our new lives of joy and peace by believing the promise-making God, and we continue to live in the same manner. A long list of fulfilled promises is present to our happy memories, awakening our gratitude and confirming our confidence. We have tested the faithfulness of our God year after year in a great many ways but always with the same result. We have gone to Him with promises of the common things of life relating to daily bread and raiment and children and home. The Lord has dealt graciously with us in these matters. We have resorted to Him concerning sickness and slander and doubt and temptation. He has never failed us. In little things He has been mindful of us: even the hairs of our head have been numbered. When it appeared very unlikely that the promise could be kept, it has been fulfilled with remarkable exactness. We have been broken down by the falseness of man, but we have exulted and do exult in the truthfulness of God. It brings the tears into our eyes to think of the startling ways in which Jehovah, our God, has decided to carry out His gracious promises.

> Thus far we prove that promise good,
> Which Jesus ratified with blood:
> Still He is faithful, wise, and just,
> And still in Him believers trust.

Let me freely speak to all who trust in the Lord. Children of God, has not your heavenly Father been true to you? Is not this your constant experience, that you are always failing, but He never fails? Well said our apostle, *"If we believe not, yet he abideth faithful: he cannot deny himself"* (2 Tim. 2:13). We may interpret divine language in its broadest sense, and we will find that the Lord's promise is kept to the utmost of its meaning. The rule of His giving is large and liberal: the promise is a great vessel, and the Lord fills it to overflowing. As the Lord in Solomon's case gave him *"as he promised him,"* so will He in every instance as long as the world exists. Reader, believe the promise, and thus prove yourself to be an inheritor of it. May the Holy Spirit lead you to do this, for Jesus' sake.

# CHAPTER THIRTEEN

# THE RULE WITHOUT EXCEPTION

## ❧ 13 ❧

# THE RULE WITHOUT EXCEPTION

*Blessed be the LORD, that hath given rest unto his people*
*Israel, according to all that he promised: there hath*
*not failed one word of all his good promise, which he*
*promised by the hand of Moses his servant.*
—1 Kings 8:56

God gives good things to men according to His promise. This is a matter of fact and not a mere opinion. We declare it and defy all the world to bring any evidence to disprove this statement.

Upon this point I am a personal witness. My experience has been long and my observation has been wide, but I have never yet met with a person who trusted God and found the Lord's promise fail him. I have seen many living men sustained under heavy trials by resting in the Word of the Lord. I have also seen many dying persons made triumphant in death by the same means. I have never met with a believer who has been made ashamed of his hope because of his temporal afflictions or with one who on his deathbed has repented of trusting in the Lord. All my observation points the other way and confirms me in the persuasion that the Lord is faithful to all who rely upon Him. I am so certain about this matter that I would be prepared to make a solemn affirmation in a court of justice. I would not utter a falsehood under the appearance of a pious fraud, but I would testify upon this important subject as an honest witness without reserve or equivocation.

I never knew a man in the pangs of death lament that he trusted the Savior. Nay, what is more, I have never heard that such a thing has happened anywhere at any time. If there had been such a case, the haters of the Gospel would have advertised it high and low. Every street would have heard the evil news. Every preacher would have been confronted with it. We would have been met with pamphlets at the door of every church and chapel reporting that such a one, who had lived a saintly life and relied on the Redeemer's merits, had discovered in his last hours that he had been duped and that the doctrine of the cross was all delusion. We challenge opponents to discover such an instance. Let them find it among rich or poor, old or young. Let the very fiend himself, if he can, bear witness to the failure of a single promise of the living God. But it has not been said that Jehovah has deceived one of His people, and it never will be said. For God is true to every word that He has ever spoken.

God never stoops to a lie. The mere supposition is blasphemous. Why should He be false? What is there about Him that could cause Him to break His word? It would be contrary to His nature. How could He be God and not be just and true? He cannot therefore violate His promise through any lack of faithfulness.

Furthermore, the omnipotent God never promises beyond His power. We frequently intend to act according to our word; however, we find ourselves mastered by overwhelming circumstances, and our promise falls to the ground because we are unable to perform it. This can never be so with the almighty God, for His ability is without limit. All things are possible with Him.

Our promise may have been made in error, and we may afterward discover that it would be wrong to do as we have said. Unlike us, God is infallible, and therefore His word will never be withdrawn upon the ground of a mistake. Infinite wisdom has set its approval upon every promise. Each word of the Lord is registered by unerring judgment and ratified by eternal truth.

The promise cannot fail because of an alteration in the divine Promiser. We change, poor, frail things that we are! But the Lord knows no variableness or any shadow of a turning. Hence His word abides forever the same. Because He does not change, His promises stand fast like the great mountains. *"Hath he said, and shall he not do it?"* (Num. 23:19). Our strong consolation rests upon the immutable things of God.

The word of the Lord cannot fall to the ground through forgetfulness on His part. With our tongues we outrun our hands. Although we are willing, we fail in the performing because other things come in and distract our attention. We forget, or we grow cold. It is never so with the faithful Promiser. His most ancient promise is still fresh in His mind, and He means it now as He did when He first uttered it. He is, in fact, always giving the promise, since there is no time with Him. The old promises of Scripture are new promises to faith. Every word still proceeds out of the mouth of the Lord to be bread for men.

Because of all this the word of the Lord deserves all faith, both implicit and explicit. We can trust men too much, but we can never do so toward God. It is the surest thing that has been or that can ever be. To believe His word is to believe what none can fairly question. Has God said it? Then so it must be. Heaven and earth will pass away, but God's word will never pass away. The laws of nature may be suspended: fire may cease to burn, and water to drown, for this would involve no unfaithfulness in God. But for His word to fail would involve a dishonoring variableness in the character and nature of the Godhead, and that can never be. Let us affirm that God is true and never allow a suspicion of His veracity to cross our minds.

The immutable word of promise is, and ever must be, the rule of God's giving. Consider a little, while I make a further observation, namely, that against this no other rule can stand. With the rule of God's promise no other law, supposed or real, can ever come into conflict.

The law of deserving is sometimes set up against this rule, but it cannot prevail. "Oh," says one, "I cannot think that God can or will save me, for there is no good thing in me!" You speak rightly, and your fear cannot be removed if God is to act toward you upon the rule of deserving. But if you believe on His Son Jesus, that rule will not operate. The Lord will act toward you according to the rule of His promise. The promise was not founded upon your merits. It was freely made, and it will be as freely kept. If you inquire how your ill deservings can be met, let me remind you of Jesus who came to save you from your sins. The boundless deservings of the Lord Jesus are set to your account, and your terrible demerits are thereby neutralized once and for all. The law of merit would sentence you to destruction as you are, but he who believes is not under law but under grace. When under grace the great Lord deals with men according to pure mercy as revealed in His promise.

Choose not to be self-righteous, or justice must condemn you. Be willing to accept salvation as a free gift bestowed through the exercise of the sovereign prerogative of God who says, *"I will have mercy on whom I will have mercy"* (Rom. 9:15). Be humbly trustful in the grace of God that is revealed in Christ Jesus, and the promise will be richly fulfilled to you.

Neither does the Lord deal with men according to the measure of their moral ability. "Oh," says the seeker, "I think I might be saved if I could make myself better, become more religious, or exercise greater faith; but I am without strength. I cannot believe; I cannot repent; I cannot do anything right!" Remember, then, that the gracious God has not promised to bless you according to the measure of your ability to serve Him, but according to the riches of His grace as declared in His Word. If His gifts were bestowed according to your spiritual strength, you would get nothing. For you can do nothing without the Lord. But as the promise is kept according to the infinity of divine grace, there can be no question cast upon it.

You do not need to stagger at the promise through unbelief but reckon that He who has promised is able also to perform. Do not limit the Holy One of Israel by dreaming that His love is bounded by your capacity. The volume of the river is not to be computed by the dryness of the desert through which it flows. There is no logical proportion between the two. Even with half an eye one can see that there is no calculating the extent of infinite love by measuring our human weakness. The operations of almighty grace are not limited by mortal strength or by lack of strength. God's power will keep God's promise.

It is not your weakness that can defeat God's promise or your strength that can fulfill the promise. He who spoke the word will Himself make it good. It is neither your business or mine to keep God's promises. That is His office and not ours. Poor helpless one, attach your heavy wagon of incapacity to the great engine of the promise, and you will be drawn along the lines of duty and blessing! Though you are more dead than alive, though you have more weakness than strength, this will not affect the certainty of the divine engagement. The power of the promise lies in Him who made the promise. Look, therefore, away from self to God. If you are faint, fall upon the bosom of the divine promise. If you count yourself dead, be buried in the grave where the bones of a promise lie, and you will be made alive as soon as you touch them. What we can or cannot do is not the question. Everything hinges upon what the Lord can do. It is enough for us to keep our own contracts without attempting to keep God's promises. I do not like my fellowman to doubt my solvency because a beggar who lives in the next street cannot pay his debts. Why, then, should I distrust the Lord because I have grave cause to distrust myself? My ability is quite another question from the faithfulness of God, and it is a pity to mix the two things. Let us not dishonor our God by dreaming that His arm has grown short because our arm has grown weak or weary.

We must not measure God by the rule of our feelings, either. We often hear the lamentation: "I do not feel that I can be saved. I do not feel that such sin as mine can be forgiven. I do not feel it possible that my hard heart can ever be softened and renewed." This is poor, foolish talk. In what way can our feelings guide us in such matters? Do you feel that the dead in their graves can be raised again? Do you even feel that the cold of winter will be followed by the heat of summer? How can you feel these things?

You believe them. To talk of feeling in the matter is absurd. Does the fainting man feel that he will revive? Is it not the nature of such a state to suggest death? Do dead bodies feel that they will have a resurrection? Feeling is out of the question.

God gave Solomon wisdom as He had promised him, and He will give you what He has promised, whatever your feelings may be. If you look through the book of Deuteronomy, you will see how often Moses used the expression *"as he...promised."* He said, *"The LORD...bless you, as he hath promised you"* (Deut. 1:11). He cannot pronounce on Israel a larger benediction. That holy man viewed the dealings of the Lord with constant admiration because they were *"as he...promised."* In our case, also, the rule of the Lord's dealings will be *"as he...promised."* Our experience of divine grace will not be "as we now feel" but *"as he...promised."*

While writing this for the comfort of others, I feel bound to confess that, personally, I am the subject of very changeful feelings. I have learned to set very small store by them, either one way or the other. Above all, I have ceased to estimate the truth of the promise by my condition of mind. Today I feel so joyful that I can dance to the tune of Miriam's tambourine. Perhaps when I wake tomorrow morning I will only be able to sigh in harmony with Jeremiah's lamentations. Has my salvation changed according to these feelings? Then it must have had a very movable foundation. Feelings are more fickle than the winds, more insubstantial than bubbles. Are these to be the gauge of divine fidelity?

States of mind more or less depend upon the condition of the liver or the stomach. Are we to judge the Lord by these? Certainly not. The state of the barometer may send our feelings up or down. Can there be much dependence upon things so changeable? God does not suspend His eternal love upon our emotions, because if He did it would be like building a temple on a wave. We are saved according to facts, not according to fancies. Certain eternal truths prove us saved or lost. Those truths are not affected by our exhilarations or depressions. My reader, do not set up your feelings as a test by which to try the truthfulness of the Lord! Such conduct is a sort of mingled insanity and wickedness. If the Lord has said the word, He will make it good, whether you feel triumphant or despondent.

Again, God will not give to us according to the rule of probabilities. It does seem very improbable that you, my friend, should be blessed by the Lord who made heaven and earth. Yet, if you trust the Lord, you are favored as surely as the Blessed Virgin herself, of whom it is said that all generations will call her blessed. For it is written,

> *Blessed is she that believed: for there shall be a performance of those things which were told her from the Lord.* (Luke 1:45)

*"O LORD of hosts, blessed is the man that trusteth in thee"* (Ps. 84:12). It may seem improbable that an old sinner, steeped in vice, would, by believing in Jesus, at once begin a new life, and yet it will be so. It

may seem very unlikely that a woman living in sin would hear the words, *"He that believeth on the Son hath everlasting life"* (John 3:36). It also seems unlikely that she should immediately lay hold upon it and at once receive everlasting life. Yet it is true, for all that. I have seen it so.

Our God is a God of wonders. Things improbable, yes, impossible, with us are everyday things with Him. He causes the camel, despite its hump, to go through the needle's eye. He calls the things that are not as though they were. Do you laugh at the very idea of your being saved? Let it not be the distrustful laugh of Sarah but the joyous expectancy of Abraham. Believe on Jesus, and you will laugh all over, inwardly and outwardly, not from incredulity but for quite another reason. When we know God we do not cease to wonder, but we begin to be at home with wonders. Believe the promise of God's grace, and, believing, you will live in a new world that will be always wonderland to you.

It is a happy thing to have such faith in God as to expect as certain that which to mere human judgment is most unlikely. *"With God all things are possible"* (Matt. 19:26). It is therefore possible that He would save every soul that believes in Jesus. The law of gravitation acts in all cases, and so does the law of divine faithfulness. There are no exceptions to the rule that God will keep His covenant. Extreme cases, difficult cases, yes, impossible cases, are included within the circle of the Lord's word, and therefore none need despair or even doubt. God's opportunity has come when man's extremity is reached. The worse the case, the more sure is it to be helped by the Lord. Oh, that you, as hopeless and helpless as you may be, would do the Lord the honor to believe Him and leave all in His hands.

How long will it be before men will trust their God? *"O thou of little faith, wherefore didst thou doubt?"* (Matt. 14:31). Oh, that we would settle it in our minds that we would never again distrust the Faithful One!

*"Let God be true, but every man a liar"* (Rom. 3:4). The Lord Himself said, *"Is the LORD's hand waxed short? thou shalt see now whether my word shall come to pass unto thee or not"* (Num. 11:23). Let not the Lord speak thus to us in anger, but let us believe and be sure that the solemn declarations of the Lord must be fulfilled. Speak no longer one to another, saying, "What is truth?" but know infallibly that the Word of the Lord is sure and endures forever.

Here is a promise for you to begin with. Test it and see if it be not true: *"Call upon me in the day of trouble: I will deliver thee"* (Ps. 50:15).

# Chapter Fourteen

# Open the Door and Enter

## ≈ 14 ≈

# OPEN THE DOOR AND ENTER

*I am the LORD God of Abraham thy father,*
*and the God of Isaac: the land whereon thou liest,*
*to thee will I give it.*
—Genesis 28:13

Timid souls find much difficulty in laying hold of the promises of God as being made to themselves. They fear that it would be presumptuous to grasp things so good and precious. As a general rule, we may consider that if we have faith to grasp a promise, that promise is ours. He who gives us the key that will fit the lock of His door intends that we open the door and enter. There can never be presumption in humbly believing God. There may be a great deal of it in daring to question His word.

We are not likely to err in trusting the promise too far. Our failure lies in lack of faith, not in excess of it. It would be hard to believe God too much.

It is dreadfully common to believe Him too little. *"According to your faith be it unto you"* (Matt. 9:29) is a benediction from which the Lord will never draw back. *"If thou canst believe, all things are possible to him that believeth"* (Mark 9:23). It is written, *"They could not enter in because of unbelief"* (Heb. 3:19). It is never said that one who entered in by faith was censured for his impertinence and driven out again.

Jacob, according to the text with which this chapter begins, took possession of the Promised Land by stretching himself upon it and going to sleep. There is no surer way of taking possession of a promise than by placing your whole weight upon it and then enjoying a hearty rest. *"The land whereon thou liest, to thee will I give it."*

How often have I found the promise true to my own self when I have accepted it as truth and acted upon it! I have stretched myself upon it as upon a couch, and left myself in the hands of the Lord. A sweet repose has crept over my spirit. Confidence in God realizes its own desires. The promise that our Lord made to those who seek favors in prayer runs thus: *"Believe that ye receive them, and ye shall have them"* (Mark 11:24). This sounds strange, but it is true. It is according to the philosophy of faith. Say, by a realizing faith, "This promise is mine," and straightaway it is yours. It is by faith that we receive promises and not by sight and sense.

The promises of God are not enclosures to be the private property of this saint or that. They are an open common for all the dwellers in the parish of Holy Faith. No doubt there are persons who would, if they could, make a freehold of the stars and a personal estate out of the sun and moon. The same greed might put a fence around the promises, but this cannot be done. This would be just like a miser who would hedge in the songbirds and claim the music of lark and thrush as his own sole inheritance. The miser might decide to keep promises all to himself. No, not the best of the saints can, even if they wished to do so, put a single word of the God of grace under lock and key. The promise is not only *"unto you, and to your children,"* but also *"to all that are afar off, even as many as the Lord our God shall call"* (Acts 2:39). What a comfort this is! Let us take up our common rights and possess by faith what the Lord has made ours by a covenant.

Words spoken to Jacob belong equally to all believers. Hosea said of him, *"Yea, he had power over the angel, and prevailed: he wept, and made supplication unto him: he found him in Bethel, and there he spake with us"* (Hos. 12:4). So Jehovah spoke with us when He spoke with the patriarch. The wonders that God displayed at the Red Sea were worked for all His people, for we read, *"There did we rejoice in him"* (Ps. 66:6). It is true we were not there, and yet the joy of Israel's victory is ours.

The apostle quoted the word of the Lord to Joshua as if it were spoken to any and every child of God: *"He hath said, I will never leave thee, nor forsake thee"* (Heb. 13:5). The fact is that no word of the Lord ends with the occasion that called it forth or spends itself in blessing the individual to whom it was first addressed. All the promises are to believers who have faith enough to embrace them and plead them at the throne of grace. What God is to one who trusts Him, He will be to all such according to their circumstances and necessities.

The Bible has its eye upon each one of us as it utters its words of grace. A Bampton lecturer has well said,

> We, ourselves, and such as we are, are the very persons whom Scripture speaks of; and to whom, as men, in every variety of persuasive form, it makes its condescending, though celestial, appeal. The point worthy of observation is to note how a book of its description and its compass should possess this versatility of power, this eye, like that of a portrait uniformly fixed upon us, turn where we will.

> Eye of God's word! Where'er we turn,
>     Ever upon us thy kind gaze
> Doth all our depths of woe discern,
>     Unravel every bosom's maze.

> What word is this? When know'st thou me?
>     All wondering cries the humbled heart,
> To hear thee that deep mystery,
>     The knowledge of itself, impart.

This unique personality of the Word to each one of a thousand generations of believers is one of its greatest charms and one of the surest proofs of its divine inspiration. We treat our Bibles not as old almanacs but as books for the present: new, fresh, adapted for the hour. Abiding sweetness dwells in undiminished freshness in the ancient words upon which our fathers fed in their day. Glory be to God, we are feasting on them still. If not, we ought to be. We can blame only ourselves if we do not!

The wells of Abraham served for Isaac and Jacob and a thousand generations. Come, let us let down our buckets and with joy draw water out of the old wells of salvation, dug in the far-off days when our fathers trusted in the Lord and He delivered them! We need not fear that we will be superstitious or credulous. The promises of the Lord are made to all who will believe them. Faith is itself a warrant for trusting. If one can trust, one may trust. After being fulfilled hundreds of times, the words of promise still stand to be yet further made good. Many times and often have we stooped down to the springhead in the meadow and gulped a cooling portion. It is just as full and free, and we may drink today with as much confidence as if we now stooped for the first time. Men do not keep their promises over and over again. It would be unreasonable to expect it of them. They are cisterns, but You, O Lord, are a fountain! All my fresh springs are in You.

Come, reader, imitate Jacob! As he laid himself down in a certain place and took of the stones of the place for his pillows, so do you. Here is the whole Bible for a couch, and here are certain promises to serve as pillows. Lay down your burdens, and yourself also, and take your rest. Behold, this Scripture and its promises are henceforth yours— *"the land whereon thou liest, to thee will I give it."*

# CHAPTER FIFTEEN

# ENDORSING THE PROMISE

# ≈ 15 ≈

# Endorsing the Promise

*I believe God, that it shall be even as it was told me.*
—Acts 27:25

P aul had received a special promise, and he openly avowed his faith in it. He believed that God would fulfill every detail of that promise. In this way he affirmed that God is true. Each one of us is bound to do this with those words of the Lord that are suitable to our case. This is what I mean by the headline—"Endorsing the Promise."

A friend gives me a check for the Orphanage, which runs thus, "Pay to the order of C. H. Spurgeon, the sum of £10." His name is good, his bank is good, but I get nothing from his kindness until I put my own name on the back of his check. It is a very simple act. I merely sign my name, and the banker pays me, but the signature cannot be dispensed with.

There are many nobler names than mine, but none of these can be used instead of my own. If I wrote the Queen's name, it would not benefit me. If the Chancellor of the Exchequer placed his signature on the back of the document, it would be in vain. I must myself affix my own name. Even so each one must personally accept, adopt, and endorse the promise of God by his own individual faith, or he will derive no benefit from it.

If you were to write Miltonic lines in honor of the bank or exceed Tennyson in verses in praise of the generous benefactor of the orphans, it would avail nothing. The choicest language of men and of angels would count for nothing. What is absolutely requisite is the personal signature of the party who is named as the receiver. However fine might be the sketch that an artistic pencil might draw upon the back of the draft, that also would be of no sort of service. The simple, self-written name is demanded, and nothing will be accepted instead of it. We must believe the promise, each one for himself, and declare that we know it to be true, or it will bring us no blessing. No good works or ceremonial performances or rapturous feelings can supply the place of a simple confidence. *"He that cometh to God must believe that he is, and that he is a rewarder of them that diligently seek him"* (Heb. 11:6). Some things may be or may not be, but this must be.

The promise may be said to run like this: "I promise to pay to the order of any sinner who will believe on Me the blessing of eternal life." The sinner must write his name on the back of the draft.

Nothing else is asked of him. He believes the promise, he goes to the throne of grace with it, and he looks to receive the mercy that it guaranteed to him. He will have that mercy. He cannot fail to do so. It is written, *"He that believeth on the Son hath everlasting life"* (John 3:36), and so it is.

Paul believed that all in the ship with him would escape because God had promised it. He accepted the promise as ample security for the fact, and acted accordingly. He was calm amid the storm. He gave his comrades discerning and sensible advice as to breaking their fast. In general, he managed matters as a man would do who was sure of a happy escape from the tempest. Thus he treated God as He should be treated, namely, with unquestioning confidence. An upright man likes to be trusted. It would grieve him if he saw that he was regarded with suspicion. Our faithful God is jealous of His honor and cannot endure it when men treat Him as if He could be false. Unbelief provokes the Lord above any other sin. It touches the apple of His eye and cuts Him to the quick. Far be it from us to perpetrate so infamous a wrong toward our heavenly Father. Let us believe Him up to the hilt, placing no bounds to our hearty reliance upon His word.

Paul openly avowed his confidence in the promise. It is well that we should do the same. Just at this time, bold, outspoken testimonies to the truth of God are greatly needed and may prove to be of sevenfold value. The air is full of doubt. Indeed, few really and substantially believe. Such a man as George Müller, who believed in God for the maintenance of two thousand children, is a rare personage. *"When the Son of man cometh, shall He find faith on the earth?"* (Luke 18:8). Therefore, let us speak out. Infidelity has defied us. Let no man's heart fail him, but let us meet the giant with the sling and stone of actual experience and unflinching witness. God does keep His promise, and we know it. We dare endorse every one of His promises. Yes, we would do it with our blood if it were necessary! The Word of the Lord endures forever, and of this we are undaunted witnesses, even all of us who are called by His name.

# CHAPTER SIXTEEN

# THE ROAD IS SURE

# ∾ 16 ∾
# THE ROAD IS SURE

*Godliness is profitable unto all things, having promise of*
*the life that now is, and of that which is to come.*
—1 Timothy 4:8

Some Christians treat religion as if it does not relate to the common things of daily life. It is to them transcendental and dreamy. It becomes rather a creation of pious fiction than a matter of fact. They believe in God, after a fashion, for things spiritual and for the life that is to be. Yet they totally forget that true godliness has the promise of the life that now is, as well as of that which is to come. To them it would seem almost a profanation to pray about the small matters of which daily life is made up. Perhaps they will be startled if I venture to suggest that this should make them question the reality of their faith. If it cannot bring them help in little troubles of life, will it support them in the greater trials of death? If it cannot profit them as to food and raiment, what can it do for them as to the immortal spirit?

In the life of Abraham, we perceive that his faith had to do with all the events of his earthly pilgrimage. It was connected with his removals from one country to another, with the separation of a nephew from his camp, with fighting against invaders, and especially with the birth of the long-promised son. No part of the patriarch's life was outside the circle of his faith in God. Toward the close of his life it is said, *"And the LORD had blessed Abraham in all things"* (Gen. 24:1), which includes the temporal as well as the spiritual.

In Jacob's case the Lord promised him bread to eat and raiment to put on and the bringing of him to his father's house in peace. All these things are of a temporal and earthly character. Assuredly these first believers did not spirit away the present blessings of the covenant or regard it as an airy, mystical matter to believe in God. One is struck with the lack of any line of demarcation between secular and sacred in their lives. They journeyed as pilgrims, fought like Crusaders, ate and drank like saints, lived as priests, and spoke as prophets. Each of these first believers viewed his life as his religion and his religion as his life. They trusted God, not merely about certain things of higher import but about everything. Hence, even a servant from one of their houses, when he was sent on an errand, prayed, *"O LORD God of my master...prosper my way which I go"* (Gen. 24:42). This was genuine faith, and it is our duty to imitate it. No longer will we allow the substance of the promise and the life of faith to evaporate in mere sentimental and visionary fancies. If trust in God is good for anything, it is good for everything within the line of the promise. It is certain that the life that now is lies within that region.

Let my reader observe and practically use such words of God as these:

> *And ye shall serve the LORD your God, and he shall bless thy bread, and thy water; and I will take sickness away from the midst of thee.* (Exod. 23:25)

> *Trust in the LORD, and do good; so shalt thou dwell in the land, and verily thou shalt be fed.* (Ps. 37:3)

> *Surely he shall deliver thee from the snare of the fowler, and from the noisome pestilence. He shall cover thee with his feathers, and under his wings shalt thou trust: his truth shall be thy shield and buckler. Thou shalt not be afraid for the terror by night; nor for the arrow that flieth by day; nor for the pestilence that walketh in darkness; nor for the destruction that wasteth at noonday. A thousand shall fall at thy side, and ten thousand at thy right hand; but it shall not come nigh thee.*
> (Ps. 91:3–7)

> *He shall deliver thee in six troubles: yea, in seven there shall no evil touch thee.* (Job 5:19)

> *He that walketh righteously, and speaketh uprightly; he that despiseth the gain of oppressions, that shaketh*

*his hands from holding of bribes, that stoppeth his ears from hearing of blood, and shutteth his eyes from seeing evil; he shall dwell on high: his place of defence shall be the munitions of rocks: bread shall be given him; his waters shall be sure.*

(Isa. 33:15–16)

*For the* LORD *God is a sun and shield: the* LORD *will give grace and glory: no good thing will he withhold from them that walk uprightly.*     (Ps. 84:11)

*No weapon that is formed against thee shall prosper; and every tongue that shall rise against thee in judgment thou shalt condemn. This is the heritage of the servants of the* LORD, *and their righteousness is of me, saith the* LORD.     (Isa. 54:17)

Our Savior intended faith to quiet our anxiety concerning daily cares, or He would not have said,

*Therefore I say unto you, Take no thought for your life, what ye shall eat, or what ye shall drink; nor yet for your body, what ye shall put on. Is not the life more than meat, and the body than raiment? Behold the fowls of the air: for they sow not, neither do they reap, nor gather into barns; yet your heavenly Father feedeth them. Are ye not much better than they?*     (Matt. 6:25–26)

What else but the exercise of faith concerning temporal things could He have meant when He used the following language:

*And seek not ye what ye shall eat, or what ye shall drink, neither be ye of doubtful mind. For all these things do the nations of the world seek after: and your Father knoweth that ye have need of these things.* (Luke 12:29–30)

Paul meant the same when he wrote,

*Be careful for nothing; but in every thing by prayer and supplication with thanksgiving let your requests be made known unto God. And the peace of God, which passeth all understanding, shall keep your hearts and minds through Christ Jesus.* (Phil. 4:6–7)

He who has gone to prepare heaven for us will not leave us without provision for the journey there. God does not give us heaven as the Pope gave England to the Spanish king—if he could get it. He makes the road sure, as well as the end. Now, our earthly necessities are as real as our spiritual ones, and we may rest sure that the Lord will supply them. He will send us those supplies in the way of promise, prayer, and faith and so make them a means of education for us. He will fit us for Canaan by the experience of the wilderness.

To suppose that temporal things are too little for our superior God is to forget that He observes the flight of sparrows and counts the hairs of His people's heads. Besides, everything is so little to Him that, if He does not care for the little, He cares for nothing. Who is to divide affairs by size or weight?

The turning point of history may be a minute circumstance. Blessed is the man to whom nothing is too small for God. Certainly nothing is too small to cause us sorrow or to involve us in peril. A man of God once lost a key. He prayed about it and found it. It was reported by him as a strange circumstance. Actually, it was nothing unusual. Some of us pray about everything and tremble if the infinitesimal things are not sanctified by the Word of God and prayer. It is not the including of trifles that is any trouble to our consciences but the omission of them. We are assured that when our Lord gave His angels charge to guard our feet from stones in the way, He placed all the details of our life under heavenly care, and we are glad to commit all things to His keeping.

It is one of the abiding miracles of the present dispensation that in Christ we have continual peace under all trials. Through Him we have power in prayer to obtain from the Lord all things necessary for this life and godliness. It has been my lot to test the Lord hundreds of times about temporal needs. I was driven to test the Lord by the care of orphans and students. Prayer has many, many times brought opportune supplies and cleared away serious difficulties. I know that faith can fill a purse, provide a meal, change a hard heart, procure a site for a building, heal sickness, quiet insubordination, and stay an epidemic.

Like money in the worldling's hand, faith in the hand of the man of God answers all things. All things in heaven and earth and under the earth answer to the command of prayer. Faith is not to be imitated by a quack or simulated by a hypocrite. Where it is real and can grasp a divine promise with firm grip, it is a great wonder-worker. How I wish that you would so believe in God as to lean upon Him in all the concerns of your life! This would lead you into a new world and bring to you such confirmatory evidence as to the truth of our holy faith that you would laugh skeptics to scorn.

Childlike faith in God provides sincere hearts with a practical prudence that I am inclined to call *sanctified common sense*. The simpleminded believer, though laughed at as an idiot, has a wisdom about him that comes from above and effectively baffles the minds of the wicked. Nothing puzzles a malicious enemy like the straightforward unguardedness of an out-and-out believer.

He who believes his God is not afraid of evil tidings because his heart has found a calm fixity in trusting in the Lord. In a thousand ways this faith sweetens, enlarges, and enriches life. Try it, dear reader, and see if it does not yield you an immeasurable wealth of blessedness! It will not save you from trouble, for the promise is, *"These things I have spoken unto you, that in me ye might have peace. In the world ye shall have tribulation: but be of good cheer; I have overcome the world"* (John 16:33), but it will cause you to glory in tribulations.

*Knowing that tribulation worketh patience; and patience, experience; and experience, hope: and hope maketh not ashamed; because the love of God*

*is shed abroad in our hearts by the Holy Ghost*
*which is given unto us.* (Rom. 5:3–5)

My faith not only flies to heaven,
    But walks with God below;
To me are all things daily given,
    While passing to and fro.

The promise speaks of worlds above,
    But not of these alone;
It feeds and clothes me now with love,
    And makes this world my own.

I trust the Lord, and He replies,
    In things both great and small.
He honors faith with prompt supplies;
    Faith honors Him in all.

# CHAPTER SEVENTEEN

# SEEKING AND FINDING

## ❧ 17 ❧

# SEEKING AND FINDING

*Thou hast promised this goodness unto thy servant.*
—2 Samuel 7:28

King David knew what the Lord had engaged to give him, and he referred to it especially in his prayer as *"this good thing"* (2 Sam. 7:28 RSV). We greatly need to be more definite in our supplications than we usually are. We pray for everything in such a way that we practically pray for nothing. It is good to know what we need. Hence our Lord said to the blind man, *"What wilt thou that I should do unto thee?"* (Mark 10:51). He wished him to be aware of his own needs and to be filled with earnest desires concerning those needs. These are valuable ingredients in the composition of prayer.

Knowing what we need, the next business is to find that the Lord has promised us this particular blessing. Then we can go to God with the utmost confidence and look for the fulfillment of

His Word. To this end we should diligently search the Scriptures. We should look much to the cases of other believers that are like our own and endeavor to light upon that particular utterance of divine grace that is suitable to ourselves in our present circumstances. The more exact the agreement of the promise to the case, the greater the comfort that it will yield. In this school the believer will learn the value of absolute, yes, of verbal inspiration. For in his own instance he may have to dwell upon so slight a matter as the number of a noun, as Paul did when quoting the promise made to Abraham: *"Now to Abraham and his seed were the promises made. He saith not, And to seeds, as of many; but as of one, And to thy seed, which is Christ"* (Gal. 3:16).

We may rest assured that somewhere in the inspired pages there is a promise fitting the occasion. The infinite wisdom of God is seen in His having given us a revelation that meets the innumerable varieties of His people's conditions. Not a single trial is overlooked, however peculiar it may be. As there is food specially adapted for every living thing upon the face of the earth, so there is suitable support for every child of God in the volume of inspiration. If we do not find a fitting promise, it is because we do not look for it or, having found it, have not yet perceived its full meaning.

A homely comparison may be useful here. You have lost the key of a chest, and, after trying all the keys you possess, you are obliged to send out for a locksmith. The tradesman comes with a huge bunch of keys of all sorts and sizes. To you they appear to be a strange collection of rusty instruments. He looks at the lock, and then he tries first one key and then another. He has not opened it yet. Your treasures are still out of your reach. Look, he has found a likely key. It almost touches the bolt but not quite. He is evidently on the right track now. At last the chest is opened, for the right key has been found.

This is a correct representation of many a perplexity. You cannot get at the difficulty so as to deal with it correctly and find your way to a happy result. You pray but do not have the liberty in prayer that you desire. A definite promise is what you need. You try one and another of the inspired words, but they do not fit. The troubled heart sees reasons to suspect that they are not strictly applicable to the case in hand, and so they are left in the old Book for use another day. They are not available in the present emergency. You try again, and in due season a promise presents itself that seems to have been made for the occasion. It fits as exactly as a well-made key fits the wards of the lock for which it was originally prepared. Having found the identical Word of the living God, you hasten to plead it at the throne of grace, saying, "O my Lord, You have promised this good thing unto Your servant; be pleased to grant it!" The matter is ended. Sorrow is turned to joy and prayer is heard.

Frequently the Holy Spirit brings to our remembrance with life and power words of the Lord that we otherwise might have forgotten. He also sheds a new light upon well-remembered passages and so reveals a fullness in them that we had little suspected. In cases known to me, the texts have been unusual, and for a while the person upon whose mind they were impressed could hardly see their bearing. For years one heart was comforted with the words, *"His soul shall dwell at ease; and his seed shall inherit the earth"* (Ps. 25:13). This passage was seldom out of his mind. Indeed, it seemed to him to be perpetually whispered in his ear. The special relation of the promise to his experience was made known by the event. A child of God, who mourned his years of barrenness, was lifted at once into joy and peace by that seldom-quoted word, *"I will restore to you the years that the locust hath eaten"* (Joel 2:25). The bitter experiences of David as to slander and malice led to the utterance of consoling promises. These promises have been a thousand times appropriated by obscure and brokenhearted Christians when afflicted with *"trial*[s] *of cruel mockings"* (Heb 11:36). Before this dispensation closes, we do not doubt that every sentence of Scripture will have been illustrated by the life of one or other of the saints. Perhaps some obscure and little-understood promise is still lying by until he for whom it was specially written comes. If we may so say, there is one rusty key on the bunch that has not yet found its lock, but it will find it before the history of the church is finished. We may be sure of that.

The Word of the Lord that would remove our present discomfort may be close at hand, and yet we may not be aware of it. With remarkable knowledge of human experience, John Bunyan represented the prisoner of Doubting Castle as finding in his own bosom the key called Promise that opened every door in that gloomy prison. We often lie in vile wait when the method of obtaining fullest liberty proffers itself to us. If we would but open our eyes, we would, like Hagar, see a well of water close at hand and wonder why we thought about dying of thirst. At this moment, tempted brother or sister, there is a word of the Lord awaiting you!

As the manna fell early in the morning and lay ready for the Israelites to gather it as soon as they left their beds, so does the promise of the Lord wait for His coming. The oxen and the fatlings of grace are killed, and all things are ready for your immediate comfort. The mountain is full of chariots of fire, and horses of fire, prepared for your deliverance. The prophet of the Lord can see them, and if your eyes were opened you would see them, too. Like the lepers at the gate of Samaria, it would be foolish for you to sit where you are and die. Awaken yourself, for close at hand lavish mercy is poured forth, exceeding abundantly above all that you do ask or even think. (See Ephesians 3:20.) Only believe and enter into rest.

For the poor, the sick, the faint, the erring, there are words of good cheer that they alone can enjoy. For the fallen, the desponding, the despairing, and the dying, there are friendly people who have a special sympathy for their particular maladies. The widow and the fatherless have their promises, and so have captives, travelers, shipwrecked mariners, aged persons, and those in the article of death. No one ever wanders where a promise does not follow him.

An atmosphere of promise surrounds believers as the air surrounds the globe. I might almost call it omnipresent and say of it, *"Thou hast beset me behind and before, and laid thine hand upon me. Such knowledge is too wonderful for me; it is high, I cannot attain unto it. Whither shall I go from thy spirit? or whither shall I flee from thy presence?"* (Ps. 139:5–7). No depth of darkness can hide us from the covenant of promise. In its presence the night shines like the day. Therefore, let us take courage and by faith and patience wait in the land of our exile until the day of our home-bringing. So we will, like the rest of the heirs of salvation, inherit the promise.

Certain covenant engagements made with the Lord Jesus Christ as to His elect and redeemed ones are altogether without condition so far as we are concerned. Many other wealthy words of the Lord contain stipulations that must be carefully regarded, or we will not obtain the blessing. One part of your diligent search must be directed toward this most important point. God will keep His promise to you. Only see to it that the way in which He conditions His engagement is carefully observed by you. Only when we fulfill the requirement of a conditional promise can we expect that promise to be fulfilled to us.

He has said, *"Whosoever shall call on the name of the Lord shall be saved"* (Acts 2:21). If you believe in the Lord Jesus Christ, it is certain that you will be saved, but not otherwise. In the same way, if the promise is made to prayer, to holiness, to reading the Word, to abiding in Christ, or whatever else it may be, give your heart and soul to the thing commanded, so that the blessing may become yours. In some cases, great blessedness is not realized because known duties are neglected. The promise cannot enter because *"sin lieth at the door"* (Gen. 4:7). Even an unknown duty may whip us with a few stripes, and a few strokes may greatly mar our happiness. Let us endeavor to know the Lord's will in all things, and then let us obey it without a trace of hesitation. It is not of the way of our willfulness but of the tracks of divine wisdom that we read, *"Her ways are ways of pleasantness, and all her paths are peace"* (Prov. 3:17).

Do not undervalue the grace of the promise because it has a condition appended to it. With this condition it is made doubly valuable. This condition is actually another blessing, which the Lord has purposely made inseparable from that which you desire. So you may gain two mercies while seeking only one. Moreover, remember that the condition is grievous to only those who are not heirs of the promise. To them it is as a thorn hedge, keeping them from the comfort to which they have no right. To you it is not grievous, but pleasant, and it is therefore no hindrance upon your access to the blessing. Those requirements, which show a black cloud and darkness to the Egyptians, have a bright side for the Israelites and give light by night to them. To us the Lord's yoke is easy, and in taking it upon us we find rest for our souls. (See Matthew 11:29–30.) See then that you note the wording of the promise and carry out all its precepts, so that all good things may come to you.

If you are a believer in the Lord Jesus, all the promises are yours. Among them is one for this very day of the month and for this particular place where you are now encamped. Therefore search the roll of your Magna Carta, and find out your portion for this hour. Of all the promises that the Lord has given in His Book, He has said, *"No one of these shall fail, none shall want her mate: for my mouth it hath commanded"* (Isa. 34:16). Therefore trust, and be not afraid. Whatever else may prove a failure, the promise of God never will. Treasure laid up in this bank is beyond all hazard. *"It is better to trust in the LORD than to put confidence in princes"* (Ps. 118:9). Let us sing at every remembrance of the God of truth and grace.

> Tell of His wondrous faithfulness,
> And sound His power abroad;
> Sing the sweet promise of His grace,
> And the performing God.
>
> He that can dash whole worlds to death,
> And make them when He please;
> He speaks, and that almighty breath
> Fulfills His great decrees.
>
> His very word of grace is strong
> As that which built the skies;
> The voice that rolls the stars along
> Speaks all the promises.

# CHAPTER EIGHTEEN

# THE TIME OF THE PROMISE

## ≈ 18 ≈

# THE TIME OF THE PROMISE

*The time of the promise drew nigh.*
—Acts 7:17

Thomas Brooks reminds us that the mercies of God are not called *swift,* but *"the sure mercies of David"* (Isa. 55:3). There is nothing of hurry about the procedure of the Lord. It may even seem that the chariots of His grace are long in coming. It is by no means an unusual circumstance for the saints to be heard crying, "O Lord, how long?" It is written, *"The glory of the LORD shall be thy rereward"* (Isa. 58:8). Now the guard of the rear comes up last, but it does come. God may sometimes make us wait, but we shall see in the end that He is as surely the Omega as the Alpha of His people's salvation. Let us never distrust Him, but *"though* [the vision] *tarry, wait for it; because it will surely come, it will not tarry"* (Hab. 2:3).

There once sailed from the port of London a vessel that the owner called the *Swift Sure* because he hoped it would prove both safe and speedy. Truly this is a fit name for the Lord's mercy because it is both swift and sure. David may not have said so in the text that Brooks quotes, but he often said as much and even more in others. Did he not say, *"He rode upon a cherub, and did fly: and he was seen upon the wings of the wind"* (2 Sam. 22:11)? The Lord is not slow to hear the cries of His people. He has a set time to favor Zion, and when that set time comes there will be no delay.

The date for its fulfillment is an important part of a promise. It enters into the essence of it. It would be unjust to delay the payment of a debt, and the obligation to keep one's word is of the same nature. The Lord is prompt to the moment in carrying out His gracious engagements. The Lord had threatened to destroy the world with a flood, but He waited the full time of respite until Noah had entered the ark. Then, on the same day, the fountains of the great deep were broken up. He had declared that Israel should come out of Egypt, and it was so:

> *And it came to pass at the end of the four hundred and thirty years, even the selfsame day it came to pass, that all the hosts of the LORD went out from the land of Egypt.* (Exod. 12:41)

According to Daniel, the Lord numbers the years of His promise and counts the weeks of His waiting. As for the greatest promise of all, namely, the sending of His Son from heaven, the Lord was not behind hand in that great gift, *"But when the fulness of the time was come, God sent forth his Son, made of a woman"* (Gal. 4:4). Beyond all question, the Lord our God keeps His word to the moment.

When we are in need, we may be urgent with the Lord to come quickly to our rescue, even as David pleaded in the seventieth Psalm, *"Make haste, O God, to deliver me; make haste to help me, O LORD"* (v. 1). *"But I am poor and needy: make haste unto me, O God: thou art my help and my deliverer; O LORD, make no tarrying"* (v. 5). The Lord even condescends to describe Himself as making speed to carry out His gracious engagements, saying, *"I the LORD will hasten it in his time"* (Isa. 60:22). But we must not pray in this fashion as though we had the slightest fear that the Lord could or would be remiss or that He needed us to quicken His diligence. No. *"The Lord is not slack concerning his promise, as some men count slackness"* (2 Pet. 3:9). Our God is slow to anger, but in deeds of grace, *"his word runneth very swiftly"* (Ps. 147:15). Sometimes His speed to bless His people outstrips time and thought: as, for instance, when He fulfills that ancient declaration, *"It shall come to pass, that before they call, I will answer; and while they are yet speaking, I will hear"* (Isa. 65:24).

Yet there are delays in the answers to our prayers. As the husbandman does not reap today what he sowed yesterday, so neither do we always at once obtain from the Lord what we seek from Him. The door of grace does open, but not to our first knocks. Why is this? It is because the mercy will be all the greater for being longer on the road. There is *"a time to every purpose under the heaven"* (Eccl. 3:1), and everything is best in its time. Fruit ripens in its season, and the more seasonable it is, the better it is. Untimely mercies would be only half mercies. Therefore, the Lord withholds them until they have come to their perfection. Even heaven itself will be all the better because it will not be ours until it is prepared for us and we are prepared for it.

Love presides over the arrangements of grace and strikes upon the bell when the best moment has arrived. God blesses us by His temporary delays as well as by His prompt replies. We are not to doubt the Lord because His time has not yet come. To doubt Him would be to act like petulant children who must have a thing at the instant or else they think they will never get it. A waiting God is the true object of confidence to His waiting people. *"Therefore will the LORD wait, that he may be gracious unto you"* (Isa. 30:18). His compassions fail not even when His gracious operations appear to be suspended and our griefs are deepened.

It is because He loves us so much that He tries us by delaying His answers of peace. It is with our Father in heaven even as it was with our Lord on earth: *"Now Jesus loved Martha, and her sister, and Lazarus. When he had heard therefore that he was sick, he abode two days still in the same place where he was"* (John 11:5–6). Love closes the hand of divine bounty and restrains the outflow of favor when it sees that a solid gain will ensue from a period of trial.

Perhaps the time of the promise has not yet come because our trial has not yet fulfilled its purpose. The chastening must answer its purpose, or it cannot be brought to an end. Who would desire to see the gold taken out of the fire before its waste is consumed? Wait, precious thing, until you have gained the utmost purity! These furnace moments are profitable. It would be unwise to shorten such golden hours. The time of the promise corresponds with the time most enriching to heart and soul.

Perhaps, moreover, we have not yet displayed sufficient submission to the divine will. Patience has not yet had her perfect work. The weaning process is not accomplished. We are still hankering after the comforts that the Lord intends us forever to outgrow. Abraham made a great feast when his son Isaac was weaned. Our heavenly Father will do the same with us. Lie down, proud heart! Quit worshipping your idols; forsake your fond dotings, and the promised peace will come to you.

Possibly, also, we have not yet performed a duty that will become the turning point of our condition. The Lord turned again the captivity of Job when he prayed for his friends. It may be that the Lord will make us useful to a relative or other friend before He will favor us with personal consolations. We are not able to see the face of Jesus, but we can see Him in our brothers. Some ordinance of the Lord's house may lie neglected, or some holy work may be left undone; this may hinder the promise. Is this so? *"Are the consolations of God small with thee? is there any secret thing with thee?"* (Job 15:11). Peradventure we are yet to vow unto the Lord and make a notable sacrifice unto Him, and then will He bring His covenant to mind. Let Him not have to complain, *"Thou hast bought me no sweet cane with money"* (Isa. 43:24). Rather let us accept His challenge, *"Bring ye all the tithes into the storehouse, that there may be meat in mine house, and prove me now herewith, saith the LORD of hosts, if I will not open you the windows of heaven, and pour you out a blessing"* (Mal. 3:10).

God's promises are dated to secure His glory in their fulfillment, and this must be enough for us when we can see no other reason for delay. It may be necessary for us to be made more fully aware of our need and the great value of the blessings that we crave. That which too lightly comes may be too lightly prized. Perhaps our ungrateful spirits need tutoring to thankfulness by an education of waiting. We might not loudly sing if we did not deeply sigh. Wanting and waiting lead to panting and pleading, and these in due time lead to joying and rejoicing.

If all things could be known to us as they are known to God, we would bless Him with all our hearts for keeping us under the smarting rod and not sparing us for our crying. If we could know the end as well as the beginning, we would praise the Lord for closed doors and frowning looks and unanswered petitions. Surely, if we knew that the Lord's great purposes were answered by our continuing without the pleasures we desire and bearing the evils that we dread, we would cry aloud to be left in our poverty and to be shut up in our pain. If we can glorify God by being denied what we seek, we desire to be denied. Greatest of all our prayers and sum of all the rest, is this one, *"Nevertheless not as I will, but as thou wilt"* (Matt. 26:39).

# CHAPTER NINETEEN

# THROUGH THE SPIRIT

# ❧ 19 ❧
# THROUGH THE SPIRIT

*That holy Spirit of promise, which is the earnest of our*
*inheritance until the redemption of the purchased*
*possession, unto the praise of his glory.*
—Ephesians 1:13–14

In a very true and real sense the things promised
in the covenant are already the property of believers. *"All things are yours"* (1 Cor. 3:21). The great
Father might truly say to each one of the sons who
abide in His house, *"All that I have is thine"* (Luke
15:31). The inheritance is already ours, say the old
divines, *in promisso, in pretio, in principiis.* It is ours
in the promise of God, in the price paid by the Lord
Jesus, and in its first principles that are infused into
us by the Holy Spirit. In His sure promise the Father
has already *"blessed us with all spiritual blessings in
heavenly places in Christ"* (Eph. 1:3). He has not only
resolved to enrich us in the future, but even now He
has endowed us with the treasures of His love. The

Lord Jesus has not merely made us heirs of an infinite estate in the ages to come, but He has brought us into immediate enjoyment of a present portion, as says the Scripture, *"In whom also we have obtained an inheritance"* (Eph. 1:11).

The Holy Spirit is in many ways the means of making the promised heritage ours even now. By Him we are sealed. We know with certainty that the inheritance is ours and that we ourselves belong to the great Heir of all things. The operations of the Holy Spirit upon us in our regeneration and His abiding in us by sanctification are certificates of our being in grace and of our being inheritors of glory. Beyond all other testimonies of our being saved, there stands this sure and certain evidence, namely, that the Spirit of the living God rests upon us. Repentance, faith, spiritual life, holy desires, upward breathings, and even *"groanings which cannot be uttered"* (Rom. 8:26) are all proofs that the Holy Spirit is working upon us. He is working in a way particular to the heirs of salvation.

Life breathed into us by the Holy Spirit is the great seal of the kingdom of God to our souls. We need no dreams, visions, mystic voices, or rapturous feelings. The quickening and renewing of the Holy Spirit are better seals than these. The Spirit of promise does not prepare men for a blessedness that will never be theirs. He who has brought us to the selfsame thing will secure upon us that blessing for which He has prepared us. The faintest impress of the seal of the Spirit is a better testimony of our part and lot with the people of God than all the presumptuous inferences that self-conceit can draw from its heated fancies.

Nor is the Holy Spirit only the seal of the inheritance; He is also the earnest of it. Now an earnest is a part of the thing itself, given as a guarantee that the remainder will be coming in due time. If a man is paid a part of his six-days' wage in the middle of the week, it is earnest money. In this, an earnest differs from a pledge, for a pledge is returned when we receive that which it secured. An earnest is not returned, for it is a part of that which is promised. Even so the Holy Spirit is Himself a great portion of the inheritance of the saints. In having Him we have the beginning of perfectness, of heaven, of eternal glory. He is everlasting life, and His gifts, graces, and workings are the first principles of endless happiness. In having the Holy Spirit we have the kingdom that is our Father's good pleasure to give to His chosen.

This will be made clear by a few moments' reflection. Heaven will much consist of holiness. It is clear that, as far as the Holy Spirit makes us holy here, He has implanted the beginnings of heaven. Heaven is victory. Each time we overcome sin, Satan, the world, and the flesh, we have foretastes of the unfading triumph that causes the waving of palms in the New Jerusalem. Heaven is an endless Sabbath. How can we a have better understanding of the perfect rest than through that joy and peace that are shed abroad in us by the Holy Spirit (Rom. 5:5)?

Communion with God is a chief ingredient in the bliss of the glorified. Here below, by the Spirit of God, we are enabled to delight ourselves in the Lord and rejoice in the God of our salvation. Fellowship with the Lord Jesus in all His gracious designs and purposes, and likeness to Him in love for God and man are also chief constituents in our perfected condition before the throne. The Spirit of holiness is working on these things in us from day to day. To be pure in heart so as to see God, to be established in character so as to be fixed in righteousness, to be strong in good so as to overcome all evil, and to be cleansed from self so as to find our all in God; are not these all part of the central benedictions of the beatific vision? And are they not already bestowed upon us by that Spirit of glory and of power that is resting on us right now? It is so. In the Holy Spirit we have the things we seek after. In Him the flower of heaven has come to us in the bud, and the dawn of the day of glory has smiled upon us.

We are not, then, such strangers to the promised blessings as common talk would make us out to be. Many repeat, like parrots, the word, *"Eye hath not seen, nor ear heard, neither have entered into the heart of man, the things which God hath prepared for them that love him"* (1 Cor. 2:9). But they fail to add the words that follow in the same Scripture, *"But God hath revealed them unto us by his Spirit"* (v. 10). What cruelty it is to cut the living child of Scripture in half! The Holy Spirit has revealed to us what neither eye nor ear has perceived. He has drawn back the curtains and asked us to see the secrets hidden from ages and from generations. Behold, the life of God is within your soul, the everlasting life that is promised to those who love God.

The life of glory is but the continuance and the outgrowth of the life of grace. Behold, in reconciliation through the atoning blood, that celestial peace that is the groundwork of eternal rest. In the love of God shed abroad in the believing soul, one can see a foretaste of the fragrance of happiness. In the immovable security and hallowed serenity of full assurance, mark a forecast of the infinite repose of paradise. When our inward joys swell high and burst into a song, then we hear preludes of the heavenly hallelujahs. We can experience Canaan because it is brought to us by those emotions and anticipations that, under the guidance of the Spirit, have gone, like spies, into the good land and brought us hence its choicest fruits!

It is not only that we will have an inheritance, but we have it now. In having the Holy Spirit, we are already put in possession of the land that flows with milk and honey. *"We which have believed do enter into rest"* (Heb. 4:3). *"Ye are come unto mount Sion, and unto the city of the living God, the heavenly Jerusalem, and to an innumerable company of angels"* (Heb. 12:22). What remains for such persons, who have been made partakers of a divine inheritance in the Son of God, but that they walk worthy of their high, holy, heavenly calling? *"If ye then be risen with Christ, seek those things which are above, where Christ sitteth on the right hand of God"* (Col. 3:1).

# CHAPTER TWENTY

# JESUS AND THE PROMISES

# ≈ 20 ≈

# JESUS AND THE PROMISES

*For all the promises of God in him are yea, and in him*
*Amen, unto the glory of God by us.*
—2 Corinthians 1:20

Jesus, our Lord, stands forever connected with the way of the promise. Indeed, He is *"the way, the truth, and the life"* (John 14:6). No man comes to the faithful Promiser but by Jesus Christ. I could not close this little book without a short chapter on Him. My hope is that you will not attempt to obtain any comfort from a word that I have written, or even from the Word of God itself, unless you receive it through Jesus Christ. Apart from Him the Scripture itself contains nothing that the soul of man may live upon. This, indeed, is the great fault of many—they search the Scriptures, for in them they think they have eternal life. They do not realize that they must come unto Christ, so that they might have life. Let us not be of this foolish company. Let us come to

Jesus day by day, knowing that *"it pleased the Father that in him should all fulness dwell"* (Col. 1:19). Only as we know Him do we know the light, life, and liberty of the heirs of promise. As surely as we wander from Him we roam into bondage. Oh, for grace to abide in Him, that we may possess all the good things of the covenant made with us in Him.

Jesus is the Gate of the promises. Through Him the Lord is able to enter into gracious engagements with guilty men. Until "the seed of the woman" had been appointed to be the Mediator between God and man, no messages of comfort could be sent to the offending race. God had no word for sinners until the Word of God undertook to be made flesh and to dwell among us. God could not communicate His mind of love to men except through Jesus, the Word. As God could not come to us apart from the Messenger of the covenant, so we could not approach Him except through the Mediator. Our fears drive us away from the Holy One until we see in the Son of God a Brother full of tender sympathy. The glory of the divine Trinity overawes us until we behold the milder radiance of the Incarnate God. We come to God through the humanity of His Son and especially through that humanity suffering and dying on our behalf.

Jesus is the Sum of all the promises. When God promised His Son to be ours, He gave us in Him all things necessary for our salvation. *"Every good gift and every perfect gift"* (James 1:17) will be found within the person, offices, and work of our Redeemer. All the promises are *"in him."* If you would add them up or make a long catalog of all the blessings that they secure for us, you may save yourself the pains and be happy to know that this is the full total—the Lord has given us His Son Jesus. As all the stars are in the sky and all the waves are in the sea, so are all covenant blessings in Christ. We cannot think of a real blessing outside our Lord; He is all in all. On this thread all pearls are strung; in this casket all gems are contained.

Jesus is the Guarantee of the promises. He who did not spare His own Son will deny nothing to His people. If He had ever thought of drawing back, He would have done so before He had made the infinite sacrifice of His only begotten Son. Never can there be a suspicion that the Lord will revoke any one of the promises since He has already fulfilled the greatest and most costly of them all. *"How shall he not with him also freely give us all things?"* (Rom. 8:32).

Jesus is the Confirmer of the promises. They are *"in him...yea, and in him Amen."* His coming into our nature, His standing as our federal Head, and His fulfilling of all the stipulations of the covenant have made all the articles of the divine compact firm and enduring. Now it is not only kind but also just with God to keep His promises to men. Since Jesus has rendered, on man's behalf, a full recompense to the divine honor that sin has assailed, the justice of God unites with His love in securing the carrying out of every word of promise. As the rainbow is our assurance that the world will never be destroyed by a flood, so is Jesus our assurance that the floods of human sin will never drown the faithful kindness of the Lord. He has magnified the law and made it honorable. He must be rewarded for His soul-travail, and therefore all good things must come to those for whom He died. It would be an unhinging and dislocation of all things if the promises were now to become of no effect after our Lord has done all that was required to make them sure. If we are indeed one with the Lord Jesus Christ, the promises are as sure to us as the love of His Father is to Him.

Jesus is the Remembrancer of the promises. He pleads with God on our behalf, and His plea is the divine promise. He *"made intercession for the transgressors"* (Isa. 53:12). For the good things that He has promised the Lord will be inquired of by us that He may do them for us. This inquiry may be carried out under the most encouraging circumstances; behold, the Lord Jesus Himself becomes the Intercessor for us. For Zion's sake He does not hold His peace, but day and night He makes remembrance of the everlasting covenant and of the blood whereby it was sealed and ratified. Behind of every promise stands the living, pleading, and prevailing High Priest of our profession. We may forget the faithful promise, but He will not. He will present the incense of His merit and the engagements of God on our behalf, in that place within the veil where He exercises omnipotent intercession.

Jesus is the Fulfiller of the promises. His first Advent brought us the major part of the blessings that the Lord has foreordained for His own, and

His second advent is to bring us the rest. Our spiritual riches are linked with His ever-worthy person. Because He lives, we live; because He reigns, we reign; because He is accepted, we are accepted. Soon, at His manifestation, we will be manifested; in His triumph, we will triumph; in His glory, we will be glorified. He is Himself the Alpha and the Omega of the promises of God. In Him we have found life as sinners; in Him we will find glory as saints. If He is not risen, our faith is vain; and if He does not come a second time, our hope is a delusion. Yet since He has risen from the dead, we are justified. Since He will come in the glory of the Father, we also will be glorified.

Reader, what will you do with Christ? All will depend upon your answer to this question. Do you rest alone in Him? Then the Lord has promised to bless you and do you good. He will surprise you with the amazing manner in which He will do this for you. Nothing is too good for the Father to give to the man who delights in His Son Jesus.

On the other hand, are you trusting in your own doings, feelings, prayings, and ceremonials? Then you are of the works of the law, and you are under the curse. See what I said of the seed of Hagar, the bondwoman, and guess what your portion will be. Oh, that you would leave the house of bondage and flee to the home of free grace and become one whom God will bless according to the promise!

God grant this great favor unto you for the Lord Jesus Christ's sake! Amen.